When The Pain Is "Unbegrieveable!"
A One-Year Grief Journey Journal

By: Lisa Mikell

Grief Hope In Him Publishing

ISBN-13: 978-1-7333734-0-1

ISBN-10: 1-7333734-0-3

Contact info:

LisaNoel@GriefHopeInHim.com

Grief Hope In Him
PO Box 930324
Rockaway Beach, NY 11693

Follow us:

Facebook @Grief Hope In Him

Instagram @GriefHopeInHim (Follow our hashtags.)

#griefhopeinhim #unbegrieveable

#whenthepainisunbegrieveable

Pinterest @Grief Hope In Him

Twitter @GriefHopeInHim

Disclaimer: While the use of this journal may be therapeutic, it does not replace the need for traditional counseling/therapy. If you are in need of counseling/therapy, please contact a professional in your area.

All biblical quotes are from the King James Bible.

Dedication

I dedicate this journal to my Heavenly Father, whose love
is greater than I'll ever know, my Lord and Savior, Jesus Christ,
my husband, Keith, my daughters, Kharissa and Ariah, my son,
Deuce, my mom, my dad (deceased), and my brothers,
Leroy and Chris (deceased).

Thank you for your love, support, patience, and inspiration.
I love you all tremendously!
XOXO

Photo Page

This grief journal is dedicated to the memory of:

Name: _____

Place a photo or a collage of
photos of your loved one here.

Memorial Page

Name of the deceased: _____

Date of birth: _____ Date of death: _____

Age at the time of death: _____

Place of death: _____

Time of death: _____

Cause of death: _____

Your relationship to the deceased: _____

Who informed you of the death? _____

Where were you? _____

What time was it? _____

What were you doing when you found out about the death? ___

_____

What were your immediate feelings when you found out? ____

_____

What did you do after you found out about the death? _____

_____

_____

_____

_____

_____

_____

_____

104 Emotions/Feelings/Moods

Below is a list of 104 feelings, emotions, and moods. Write the dominate one on the top of your journal page for that day. If you don't see one here, please feel free to use your own.

Abandoned Afraid Agitated Amazed Angry Annoyed

Anticipating Anxious Appreciated Apprehension Ashamed Bitter

Blessed Bored Calm Cautious Confused Content Creative Denial

Depressed Desperate Determined Disappointed Disbelief

Disconnected Disturbed Embarrassed Emotional Empowered

Empty Excited Exhausted Faithful Fearful Focused Forgiving

Forgotten Frustrated Glad Gloomy Grateful Grieving Guilty

Happy Heartbroken Hesitant Hopeful Hopeless Humiliated Hurt

Indecisive Inspired Irritated Jealous Joyful Judged Lonely Lost

Loved Mad Miserable Misunderstood Motivated Mournful

Nervous Numb Optimistic Outraged Overwhelmed Peaceful

Pessimistic Powerful Powerless Recovering Refreshed Regret

Relaxed Relieved Renewed Resentful Sad Safe Scared Sensitive

Shocked Sorrowful Strengthened Strong Surprised Terrified

Thankful Tired Uncertain Uncomfortable Understood Uninspired

Upset Useless Vulnerable Weak Withdrawn Worried Worthless

Monthly Motivation #1

1 Thessalonians 4:13-14 13. But I would not have you to be ignorant, brethren, concerning them which are asleep, that ye sorrow not, even as others which have no hope. 14. For if we believe that Jesus died and rose again, even so them also which sleep in Jesus will God bring with Him.

~KJV

Today's Date: _____

What is your grief level from 0-10, with ten being the strongest? _____

What is your dominate feeling, emotion, or mood today?
_____

What are your thoughts today?

_____
_____
_____
_____
_____
_____
_____
_____
_____
_____
_____
_____
_____
_____
_____
_____
_____
_____
_____
_____
_____
_____
_____
_____
_____
_____
_____
_____

Today's Date: _____

What is your grief level from 0-10, with ten being the strongest? _____

What is your dominate felling, emotion, or mood today?
_____

What are your thoughts today?

_____
_____
_____
_____
_____
_____
_____
_____
_____
_____
_____
_____
_____
_____
_____
_____
_____
_____
_____
_____
_____
_____
_____
_____
_____
_____
_____
_____
_____

Today's Date: _____

What is your grief level from 0-10, with ten being the strongest? _____

What is your dominate feeling, emotion, or mood today? _____

What are your thoughts today?

_____
_____
_____
_____
_____
_____
_____
_____
_____
_____
_____
_____
_____
_____
_____
_____
_____
_____
_____
_____
_____
_____
_____
_____
_____
_____
_____
_____
_____
_____

Today's Date: _____

What is your grief level from 0-10, with ten being the strongest? _____

What is your dominate felling, emotion, or mood today?
_____

What are your thoughts today?

_____
_____
_____
_____
_____
_____
_____
_____
_____
_____
_____
_____
_____
_____
_____
_____
_____
_____
_____
_____
_____
_____
_____
_____
_____
_____
_____
_____
_____
_____

Today's Date: _____

What is your grief level from 0-10, with ten being the
strongest? _____

What is your dominate feeling, emotion, or mood today?
_____

What are your thoughts today?

_____
_____
_____
_____
_____
_____
_____
_____
_____
_____
_____
_____
_____
_____
_____
_____
_____
_____
_____
_____
_____
_____
_____
_____
_____
_____
_____
_____
_____

Today's Date: _____

What is your grief level from 0-10, with ten being the strongest? _____

What is your dominate felling, emotion, or mood today?

_____

What are your thoughts today?

_____

_____

_____

_____

_____

_____

_____

_____

_____

_____

_____

_____

_____

_____

_____

_____

_____

_____

_____

_____

_____

_____

_____

_____

_____

_____

_____

Today's Date: _____

What is your grief level from 0-10, with ten being the strongest? _____

What is your dominate feeling, emotion, or mood today?
_____

What are your thoughts today?

_____
_____
_____
_____
_____
_____
_____
_____
_____
_____
_____
_____
_____
_____
_____
_____
_____
_____
_____
_____
_____
_____
_____
_____
_____
_____
_____
_____
_____

Today's Date: _____

What is your grief level from 0-10, with ten being the strongest? _____

What is your dominate felling, emotion, or mood today?
_____

What are your thoughts today?

_____

_____

_____

_____

_____

_____

_____

_____

_____

_____

_____

_____

_____

_____

_____

_____

_____

_____

_____

_____

_____

_____

_____

_____

_____

_____

_____

_____

Today's Date: _____

What is your grief level from 0-10, with ten being the strongest? _____

What is your dominate feeling, emotion, or mood today?
_____

What are your thoughts today?

_____
_____
_____
_____
_____
_____
_____
_____
_____
_____
_____
_____
_____
_____
_____
_____
_____
_____
_____
_____
_____
_____
_____
_____
_____
_____
_____
_____
_____

Today's Date: _____

What is your grief level from 0-10, with ten being the strongest? _____

What is your dominate felling, emotion, or mood today?
_____

What are your thoughts today?

_____

_____

_____

_____

_____

_____

_____

_____

_____

_____

_____

_____

_____

_____

_____

_____

_____

_____

_____

_____

_____

_____

_____

_____

_____

_____

_____

Today's Date: _____

What is your grief level from 0-10, with ten being the strongest? _____

What is your dominate feeling, emotion, or mood today?
_____

What are your thoughts today?

_____
_____
_____
_____
_____
_____
_____
_____
_____
_____
_____
_____
_____
_____
_____
_____
_____
_____
_____
_____
_____
_____
_____
_____
_____
_____
_____
_____
_____

Today's Date: _____

What is your grief level from 0-10, with ten being the strongest? _____

What is your dominate feeling, emotion, or mood today?
_____

What are your thoughts today?

_____
_____
_____
_____
_____
_____
_____
_____
_____
_____
_____
_____
_____
_____
_____
_____
_____
_____
_____
_____
_____
_____
_____
_____
_____
_____
_____
_____

Today's Date: _____

What is your grief level from 0-10, with ten being the strongest? _____

What is your dominate feeling, emotion, or mood today? _____

What are your thoughts today?

_____
_____
_____
_____
_____
_____
_____
_____
_____
_____
_____
_____
_____
_____
_____
_____
_____
_____
_____
_____
_____
_____
_____
_____
_____
_____
_____
_____
_____

Today's Date: _____

What is your grief level from 0-10, with ten being the strongest? _____

What is your dominate feeling, emotion, or mood today?

_____

What are your thoughts today?

_____
_____
_____
_____
_____
_____
_____
_____
_____
_____
_____
_____
_____
_____
_____
_____
_____
_____
_____
_____
_____
_____
_____
_____
_____
_____
_____
_____
_____
_____

Today's Date: _____

What is your grief level from 0-10, with ten being the strongest? _____

What is your dominate feeling, emotion, or mood today?
_____

What are your thoughts today?

_____
_____
_____
_____
_____
_____
_____
_____
_____
_____
_____
_____
_____
_____
_____
_____
_____
_____
_____
_____
_____
_____
_____
_____
_____
_____
_____
_____
_____

Today's Date: _____

What is your grief level from 0-10, with ten being the strongest? _____

What is your dominate feeling, emotion, or mood today? _____

What are your thoughts today?

_____
_____
_____
_____
_____
_____
_____
_____
_____
_____
_____
_____
_____
_____
_____
_____
_____
_____
_____
_____
_____
_____
_____
_____
_____
_____
_____

Today's Date: _____

What is your grief level from 0-10, with ten being the strongest? _____

What is your dominate feeling, emotion, or mood today? _____

What are your thoughts today?

_____
_____
_____
_____
_____
_____
_____
_____
_____
_____
_____
_____
_____
_____
_____
_____
_____
_____
_____
_____
_____
_____
_____
_____
_____
_____
_____
_____
_____

Today's Date: _____

What is your grief level from 0-10, with ten being the
strongest? _____

What is your dominate feeling, emotion, or mood today?
_____

What are your thoughts today?

_____
_____
_____
_____
_____
_____
_____
_____
_____
_____
_____
_____
_____
_____
_____
_____
_____
_____
_____
_____
_____
_____
_____
_____
_____
_____
_____
_____
_____

Today's Date: _____

What is your grief level from 0-10, with ten being the strongest? _____

What is your dominate feeling, emotion, or mood today?
_____

What are your thoughts today?

_____
_____
_____
_____
_____
_____
_____
_____
_____
_____
_____
_____
_____
_____
_____
_____
_____
_____
_____
_____
_____
_____
_____
_____
_____
_____
_____
_____

Today's Date: _____

What is your grief level from 0-10, with ten being the strongest? _____

What is your dominate feeling, emotion, or mood today?
_____

What are your thoughts today?

_____
_____
_____
_____
_____
_____
_____
_____
_____
_____
_____
_____
_____
_____
_____
_____
_____
_____
_____
_____
_____
_____
_____
_____
_____
_____
_____

Today's Date: _____

What is your grief level from 0-10, with ten being the strongest? _____

What is your dominate feeling, emotion, or mood today?
_____

What are your thoughts today?

_____
_____
_____
_____
_____
_____
_____
_____
_____
_____
_____
_____
_____
_____
_____
_____
_____
_____
_____
_____
_____
_____
_____
_____
_____
_____
_____

Today's Date: _____

What is your grief level from 0-10, with ten being the strongest? _____

What is your dominate feeling, emotion, or mood today?
_____

What are your thoughts today?

_____
_____
_____
_____
_____
_____
_____
_____
_____
_____
_____
_____
_____
_____
_____
_____
_____
_____
_____
_____
_____
_____
_____
_____
_____
_____
_____
_____
_____

Today's Date: _____

What is your grief level from 0-10, with ten being the strongest? _____

What is your dominate feeling, emotion, or mood today?
_____

What are your thoughts today?

_____
_____
_____
_____
_____
_____
_____
_____
_____
_____
_____
_____
_____
_____
_____
_____
_____
_____
_____
_____
_____
_____
_____
_____
_____
_____
_____
_____
_____

Today's Date: _____

What is your grief level from 0-10, with ten being the strongest? _____

What is your dominate feeling, emotion, or mood today?
_____

What are your thoughts today?

_____
_____
_____
_____
_____
_____
_____
_____
_____
_____
_____
_____
_____
_____
_____
_____
_____
_____
_____
_____
_____
_____
_____
_____
_____
_____
_____
_____

Today's Date: _____

What is your grief level from 0-10, with ten being the strongest? _____

What is your dominate feeling, emotion, or mood today?
_____

What are your thoughts today?

_____
_____
_____
_____
_____
_____
_____
_____
_____
_____
_____
_____
_____
_____
_____
_____
_____
_____
_____
_____
_____
_____
_____
_____
_____
_____
_____
_____
_____
_____

Today's Date: _____

What is your grief level from 0-10, with ten being the strongest? _____

What is your dominate feeling, emotion, or mood today? _____

What are your thoughts today?

_____
_____
_____
_____
_____
_____
_____
_____
_____
_____
_____
_____
_____
_____
_____
_____
_____
_____
_____
_____
_____
_____
_____
_____
_____
_____
_____
_____
_____

Today's Date: _____

What is your grief level from 0-10, with ten being the strongest? _____

What is your dominate feeling, emotion, or mood today?
_____

What are your thoughts today?

_____
_____
_____
_____
_____
_____
_____
_____
_____
_____
_____
_____
_____
_____
_____
_____
_____
_____
_____
_____
_____
_____
_____
_____
_____
_____
_____
_____

Today's Date: _____

What is your grief level from 0-10, with ten being the strongest? _____

What is your dominate feeling, emotion, or mood today?
_____

What are your thoughts today?

_____

_____

_____

_____

_____

_____

_____

_____

_____

_____

_____

_____

_____

_____

_____

_____

_____

_____

_____

_____

_____

_____

_____

_____

_____

_____

_____

_____

_____

_____

_____

Today's Date: _____

What is your grief level from 0-10, with ten being the strongest? _____

What is your dominate feeling, emotion, or mood today? _____

What are your thoughts today?

_____
_____
_____
_____
_____
_____
_____
_____
_____
_____
_____
_____
_____
_____
_____
_____
_____
_____
_____
_____
_____
_____
_____
_____
_____
_____
_____
_____
_____

Today's Date: _____

What is your grief level from 0-10, with ten being the
strongest? _____

What is your dominate feeling, emotion, or mood today?
_____

What are your thoughts today?

_____
_____
_____
_____
_____
_____
_____
_____
_____
_____
_____
_____
_____
_____
_____
_____
_____
_____
_____
_____
_____
_____
_____
_____
_____
_____
_____
_____
_____

Today's Date: _____

What is your grief level from 0-10, with ten being the strongest? _____

What is your dominate feeling, emotion, or mood today? _____

What are your thoughts today?

_____

_____

_____

_____

_____

_____

_____

_____

_____

_____

_____

_____

_____

_____

_____

_____

_____

_____

_____

_____

_____

_____

_____

_____

_____

Ecclesiastes 3:1-2 1.To everything there is a season, and a time to every purpose under the heaven: 2. A time to be born, and a time to die, a time to plant, and a time to pluck up that which is planted.

~KJV

Today's Date: _____

What is your grief level from 0-10, with ten being the strongest? _____

What is your dominate feeling, emotion, or mood today? _____

What are your thoughts today?

_____

_____

_____

_____

_____

_____

_____

_____

_____

_____

_____

_____

_____

_____

_____

_____

_____

_____

_____

_____

_____

_____

_____

_____

_____

_____

_____

_____

_____

_____

Today's Date: _____

What is your grief level from 0-10, with ten being the strongest? _____

What is your dominate felling, emotion, or mood today? _____

What are your thoughts today?

_____
_____
_____
_____
_____
_____
_____
_____
_____
_____
_____
_____
_____
_____
_____
_____
_____
_____
_____
_____
_____
_____
_____
_____
_____
_____
_____

Today's Date: _____

What is your grief level from 0-10, with ten being the strongest? _____

What is your dominate feeling, emotion, or mood today? _____

What are your thoughts today?

_____
_____
_____
_____
_____
_____
_____
_____
_____
_____
_____
_____
_____
_____
_____
_____
_____
_____
_____
_____
_____
_____
_____
_____
_____
_____

Today's Date: _____

What is your grief level from 0-10, with ten being the strongest? _____

What is your dominate felling, emotion, or mood today? _____

What are your thoughts today?

_____

_____

_____

_____

_____

_____

_____

_____

_____

_____

_____

_____

_____

_____

_____

_____

_____

_____

_____

_____

_____

_____

_____

_____

_____

_____

_____

_____

Today's Date: _____

What is your grief level from 0-10, with ten being the strongest? _____

What is your dominate feeling, emotion, or mood today? _____

What are your thoughts today?

_____

_____

_____

_____

_____

_____

_____

_____

_____

_____

_____

_____

_____

_____

_____

_____

_____

_____

_____

_____

_____

_____

_____

_____

_____

_____

Today's Date: _____

What is your grief level from 0-10, with ten being the strongest? _____

What is your dominate felling, emotion, or mood today? _____

What are your thoughts today?

_____
_____
_____
_____
_____
_____
_____
_____
_____
_____
_____
_____
_____
_____
_____
_____
_____
_____
_____
_____
_____
_____
_____
_____
_____
_____
_____

Today's Date: _____

What is your grief level from 0-10, with ten being the strongest? _____

What is your dominate feeling, emotion, or mood today? _____

What are your thoughts today?

_____
_____
_____
_____
_____
_____
_____
_____
_____
_____
_____
_____
_____
_____
_____
_____
_____
_____
_____
_____
_____
_____
_____
_____
_____
_____
_____
_____
_____

Today's Date: _____

What is your grief level from 0-10, with ten being the strongest? _____

What is your dominate felling, emotion, or mood today? _____

What are your thoughts today?

_____
_____
_____
_____
_____
_____
_____
_____
_____
_____
_____
_____
_____
_____
_____
_____
_____
_____
_____
_____
_____
_____
_____
_____
_____
_____
_____
_____

Today's Date: _____

What is your grief level from 0-10, with ten being the strongest? _____

What is your dominate feeling, emotion, or mood today?
_____

What are your thoughts today?

_____
_____
_____
_____
_____
_____
_____
_____
_____
_____
_____
_____
_____
_____
_____
_____
_____
_____
_____
_____
_____
_____

Today's Date: _____

What is your grief level from 0-10, with ten being the strongest? _____

What is your dominate felling, emotion, or mood today? _____

What are your thoughts today?

_____
_____
_____
_____
_____
_____
_____
_____
_____
_____
_____
_____
_____
_____
_____
_____
_____
_____
_____
_____
_____
_____
_____
_____
_____
_____

Today's Date: _____

What is your grief level from 0-10, with ten being the strongest? _____

What is your dominate feeling, emotion, or mood today? _____

What are your thoughts today?

_____

_____

_____

_____

_____

_____

_____

_____

_____

_____

_____

_____

_____

_____

_____

_____

_____

_____

_____

_____

_____

_____

_____

_____

_____

_____

_____

_____

Today's Date: _____

What is your grief level from 0-10, with ten being the strongest? _____

What is your dominate feeling, emotion, or mood today? _____

What are your thoughts today?

_____
_____
_____
_____
_____
_____
_____
_____
_____
_____
_____
_____
_____
_____
_____
_____
_____
_____
_____
_____
_____
_____
_____
_____
_____
_____
_____
_____

Today's Date: _____

What is your grief level from 0-10, with ten being the strongest? _____

What is your dominate feeling, emotion, or mood today? _____

What are your thoughts today?

_____
_____
_____
_____
_____
_____
_____
_____
_____
_____
_____
_____
_____
_____
_____
_____
_____
_____
_____
_____
_____
_____
_____
_____
_____
_____
_____

Today's Date: _____

What is your grief level from 0-10, with ten being the strongest? _____

What is your dominate feeling, emotion, or mood today? _____

What are your thoughts today?

_____
_____
_____
_____
_____
_____
_____
_____
_____
_____
_____
_____
_____
_____
_____
_____
_____
_____
_____
_____
_____
_____
_____
_____
_____
_____
_____

Today's Date: _____

What is your grief level from 0-10, with ten being the strongest? _____

What is your dominate feeling, emotion, or mood today? _____

What are your thoughts today?

_____
_____
_____
_____
_____
_____
_____
_____
_____
_____
_____
_____
_____
_____
_____
_____
_____
_____
_____
_____
_____
_____
_____
_____
_____
_____
_____
_____

Today's Date: _____

What is your grief level from 0-10, with ten being the strongest? _____

What is your dominate feeling, emotion, or mood today? _____

What are your thoughts today?

_____
_____
_____
_____
_____
_____
_____
_____
_____
_____
_____
_____
_____
_____
_____
_____
_____
_____
_____
_____
_____
_____
_____
_____
_____
_____

Today's Date: _____

What is your grief level from 0-10, with ten being the strongest? _____

What is your dominate feeling, emotion, or mood today? _____

What are your thoughts today?

_____
_____
_____
_____
_____
_____
_____
_____
_____
_____
_____
_____
_____
_____
_____
_____
_____
_____
_____
_____
_____
_____
_____
_____
_____
_____
_____

Today's Date: _____

What is your grief level from 0-10, with ten being the strongest? _____

What is your dominate feeling, emotion, or mood today? _____

What are your thoughts today?

_____
_____
_____
_____
_____
_____
_____
_____
_____
_____
_____
_____
_____
_____
_____
_____
_____
_____
_____
_____
_____
_____
_____
_____
_____

Today's Date: _____

What is your grief level from 0-10, with ten being the strongest? _____

What is your dominate feeling, emotion, or mood today? _____

What are your thoughts today?

_____
_____
_____
_____
_____
_____
_____
_____
_____
_____
_____
_____
_____
_____
_____
_____
_____
_____
_____
_____
_____
_____
_____
_____
_____
_____
_____

Today's Date: _____

What is your grief level from 0-10, with ten being the strongest? _____

What is your dominate feeling, emotion, or mood today? _____

What are your thoughts today?

_____
_____
_____
_____
_____
_____
_____
_____
_____
_____
_____
_____
_____
_____
_____
_____
_____
_____
_____
_____
_____
_____
_____
_____
_____
_____
_____
_____

Today's Date: _____

What is your grief level from 0-10, with ten being the strongest? _____

What is your dominate feeling, emotion, or mood today? _____

What are your thoughts today?

_____

_____

_____

_____

Today's Date: _____

What is your grief level from 0-10, with ten being the strongest? _____

What is your dominate feeling, emotion, or mood today? _____

What are your thoughts today?

_____

_____

_____

_____

_____

_____

_____

_____

_____

_____

_____

_____

_____

_____

_____

_____

_____

_____

_____

_____

_____

_____

_____

_____

_____

Today's Date: _____

What is your grief level from 0-10, with ten being the
strongest? _____

What is your dominate feeling, emotion, or mood today?
_____

What are your thoughts today?

_____
_____
_____
_____
_____
_____
_____
_____
_____
_____
_____
_____
_____
_____
_____
_____
_____
_____
_____
_____
_____
_____
_____
_____
_____
_____

Today's Date: _____

What is your grief level from 0-10, with ten being the strongest? _____

What is your dominate feeling, emotion, or mood today? _____

What are your thoughts today?

_____
_____
_____
_____
_____
_____
_____
_____
_____
_____
_____
_____
_____
_____
_____
_____
_____
_____
_____
_____
_____
_____
_____
_____
_____

Today's Date: _____

What is your grief level from 0-10, with ten being the strongest? _____

What is your dominate feeling, emotion, or mood today? _____

What are your thoughts today?

_____
_____
_____
_____
_____
_____
_____
_____
_____
_____
_____
_____
_____
_____
_____
_____
_____
_____
_____
_____
_____
_____
_____
_____
_____
_____
_____

Today's Date: _____

What is your grief level from 0-10, with ten being the strongest? _____

What is your dominate feeling, emotion, or mood today? _____

What are your thoughts today?

_____
_____
_____
_____
_____
_____
_____
_____
_____
_____
_____
_____
_____
_____
_____
_____
_____
_____
_____
_____
_____
_____
_____
_____
_____
_____

Today's Date: _____

What is your grief level from 0-10, with ten being the strongest? _____

What is your dominate feeling, emotion, or mood today? _____

What are your thoughts today?

_____

_____

_____

_____

_____

_____

_____

_____

_____

_____

_____

_____

_____

_____

_____

_____

_____

_____

_____

_____

_____

_____

_____

_____

_____

_____

Today's Date: _____

What is your grief level from 0-10, with ten being the strongest? _____

What is your dominate feeling, emotion, or mood today? _____

What are your thoughts today?

_____
_____
_____
_____
_____
_____
_____
_____
_____
_____
_____
_____
_____
_____
_____
_____
_____
_____
_____
_____
_____
_____
_____
_____
_____
_____
_____

Today's Date: _____

What is your grief level from 0-10, with ten being the strongest? _____

What is your dominate feeling, emotion, or mood today? _____

What are your thoughts today?

_____
_____
_____
_____
_____
_____
_____
_____
_____
_____
_____
_____
_____
_____
_____
_____
_____
_____
_____
_____
_____
_____
_____
_____
_____
_____
_____
_____

Today's Date: _____

What is your grief level from 0-10, with ten being the strongest? _____

What is your dominate feeling, emotion, or mood today? _____

What are your thoughts today?

_____
_____
_____
_____
_____
_____
_____
_____
_____
_____
_____
_____
_____
_____
_____
_____
_____
_____
_____
_____
_____
_____
_____
_____
_____
_____
_____
_____

Today's Date: _____

What is your grief level from 0-10, with ten being the strongest? _____

What is your dominate feeling, emotion, or mood today? _____

What are your thoughts today?

_____

_____

_____

_____

_____

_____

_____

_____

_____

_____

_____

_____

_____

_____

_____

_____

_____

_____

_____

_____

_____

_____

_____

_____

_____

_____

_____

_____

Romans 8:28 And we know that all things work together for good to them that love God, to them who are the called according to His purpose.

~KJV

Today's Date: _____

What is your grief level from 0-10, with ten being the
strongest? _____

What is your dominate feeling, emotion, or mood today?
_____

What are your thoughts today?

_____
_____
_____
_____
_____
_____
_____
_____
_____
_____
_____
_____
_____
_____
_____
_____
_____
_____
_____
_____
_____
_____
_____
_____
_____
_____
_____
_____

Today's Date: _____

What is your grief level from 0-10, with ten being the strongest? _____

What is your dominate felling, emotion, or mood today?
_____

What are your thoughts today?

_____
_____
_____
_____
_____
_____
_____
_____
_____
_____
_____
_____
_____
_____
_____
_____
_____
_____
_____
_____
_____
_____
_____
_____
_____
_____
_____
_____
_____

Today's Date: _____

What is your grief level from 0-10, with ten being the strongest? _____

What is your dominate feeling, emotion, or mood today?
_____

What are your thoughts today?

_____
_____
_____
_____
_____
_____
_____
_____
_____
_____
_____
_____
_____
_____
_____
_____
_____
_____
_____
_____
_____
_____
_____
_____
_____
_____
_____

Today's Date: _____

What is your grief level from 0-10, with ten being the strongest? _____

What is your dominate felling, emotion, or mood today?
_____

What are your thoughts today?

_____
_____
_____
_____
_____
_____
_____
_____
_____
_____
_____
_____
_____
_____
_____
_____
_____
_____
_____
_____
_____
_____
_____
_____
_____
_____
_____
_____
_____

Today's Date: _____

What is your grief level from 0-10, with ten being the strongest? _____

What is your dominate feeling, emotion, or mood today?
_____

What are your thoughts today?

_____
_____
_____
_____
_____
_____
_____
_____
_____
_____
_____
_____
_____
_____
_____
_____
_____
_____
_____
_____
_____
_____
_____
_____
_____
_____
_____
_____
_____

Today's Date: _____

What is your grief level from 0-10, with ten being the strongest? _____

What is your dominate felling, emotion, or mood today?
_____

What are your thoughts today?

_____

_____

_____

_____

_____

_____

_____

_____

_____

_____

_____

_____

_____

_____

_____

_____

_____

_____

_____

_____

_____

_____

_____

_____

_____

_____

_____

Today's Date: _____

What is your grief level from 0-10, with ten being the strongest? _____

What is your dominate feeling, emotion, or mood today?
_____

What are your thoughts today?

_____
_____
_____
_____
_____
_____
_____
_____
_____
_____
_____
_____
_____
_____
_____
_____
_____
_____
_____
_____
_____
_____
_____
_____
_____
_____
_____
_____

Today's Date: _____

What is your grief level from 0-10, with ten being the strongest? _____

What is your dominate felling, emotion, or mood today? _____

What are your thoughts today?

_____

_____

_____

_____

_____

_____

_____

_____

_____

_____

_____

_____

_____

_____

_____

_____

_____

_____

_____

_____

_____

_____

_____

_____

_____

_____

_____

_____

_____

Today's Date: _____

What is your grief level from 0-10, with ten being the
strongest? _____

What is your dominate feeling, emotion, or mood today?
_____

What are your thoughts today?

_____
_____
_____
_____
_____
_____
_____
_____
_____
_____
_____
_____
_____
_____
_____
_____
_____
_____
_____
_____
_____
_____
_____
_____
_____
_____
_____
_____

Today's Date: _____

What is your grief level from 0-10, with ten being the strongest? _____

What is your dominate felling, emotion, or mood today?

_____

What are your thoughts today?

_____

_____

_____

_____

_____

_____

_____

_____

_____

_____

_____

_____

_____

_____

_____

_____

_____

_____

_____

_____

_____

_____

_____

_____

_____

_____

_____

_____

Today's Date: _____

What is your grief level from 0-10, with ten being the strongest? _____

What is your dominate feeling, emotion, or mood today? _____

What are your thoughts today?

_____
_____
_____
_____
_____
_____
_____
_____
_____
_____
_____
_____
_____
_____
_____
_____
_____
_____
_____
_____
_____
_____
_____
_____
_____
_____
_____

Today's Date: _____

What is your grief level from 0-10, with ten being the strongest? _____

What is your dominate feeling, emotion, or mood today?

_____

What are your thoughts today?

_____

_____

_____

_____

_____

_____

_____

_____

_____

_____

_____

_____

_____

_____

_____

_____

_____

_____

_____

_____

_____

_____

_____

_____

_____

_____

_____

_____

Today's Date: _____

What is your grief level from 0-10, with ten being the strongest? _____

What is your dominate feeling, emotion, or mood today?
_____

What are your thoughts today?

_____
_____
_____
_____
_____
_____
_____
_____
_____
_____
_____
_____
_____
_____
_____
_____
_____
_____
_____
_____
_____
_____
_____
_____
_____
_____
_____
_____

Today's Date: _____

What is your grief level from 0-10, with ten being the strongest? _____

What is your dominate feeling, emotion, or mood today?
_____

What are your thoughts today?

_____
_____
_____
_____
_____
_____
_____
_____
_____
_____
_____
_____
_____
_____
_____
_____
_____
_____
_____
_____
_____
_____
_____
_____
_____
_____
_____
_____
_____
_____

Today's Date: _____

What is your grief level from 0-10, with ten being the
strongest? _____

What is your dominate feeling, emotion, or mood today?
_____

What are your thoughts today?

_____
_____
_____
_____
_____
_____
_____
_____
_____
_____
_____
_____
_____
_____
_____
_____
_____
_____
_____
_____
_____
_____
_____
_____
_____
_____
_____
_____
_____

Today's Date: _____

What is your grief level from 0-10, with ten being the strongest? _____

What is your dominate feeling, emotion, or mood today?
_____

What are your thoughts today?

_____
_____
_____
_____
_____
_____
_____
_____
_____
_____
_____
_____
_____
_____
_____
_____
_____
_____
_____
_____
_____
_____
_____
_____
_____
_____
_____
_____
_____
_____

Today's Date: _____

What is your grief level from 0-10, with ten being the strongest? _____

What is your dominate feeling, emotion, or mood today?
_____

What are your thoughts today?

_____
_____
_____
_____
_____
_____
_____
_____
_____
_____
_____
_____
_____
_____
_____
_____
_____
_____
_____
_____
_____
_____
_____
_____
_____
_____
_____
_____

Today's Date: _____

What is your grief level from 0-10, with ten being the strongest? _____

What is your dominate feeling, emotion, or mood today?

_____

What are your thoughts today?

_____

_____

_____

_____

_____

_____

_____

_____

_____

_____

_____

_____

_____

_____

_____

_____

_____

_____

_____

_____

_____

_____

_____

_____

_____

_____

_____

_____

_____

Today's Date: _____

What is your grief level from 0-10, with ten being the
strongest? _____

What is your dominate feeling, emotion, or mood today?
_____

What are your thoughts today?

_____
_____
_____
_____
_____
_____
_____
_____
_____
_____
_____
_____
_____
_____
_____
_____
_____
_____
_____
_____
_____
_____
_____
_____
_____
_____
_____
_____
_____

Today's Date: _____

What is your grief level from 0-10, with ten being the strongest? _____

What is your dominate feeling, emotion, or mood today? _____

What are your thoughts today?

_____

_____

_____

_____

_____

_____

_____

_____

_____

_____

_____

_____

_____

_____

_____

_____

_____

_____

_____

_____

_____

_____

_____

_____

_____

_____

_____

_____

_____

Today's Date: _____

What is your grief level from 0-10, with ten being the
strongest? _____

What is your dominate feeling, emotion, or mood today?
_____

What are your thoughts today?

_____
_____
_____
_____
_____
_____
_____
_____
_____
_____
_____
_____
_____
_____
_____
_____
_____
_____
_____
_____
_____
_____
_____
_____
_____
_____
_____
_____
_____

Today's Date: _____

What is your grief level from 0-10, with ten being the strongest? _____

What is your dominate feeling, emotion, or mood today?
_____

What are your thoughts today?

_____
_____
_____
_____
_____
_____
_____
_____
_____
_____
_____
_____
_____
_____
_____
_____
_____
_____
_____
_____
_____
_____
_____
_____
_____
_____
_____
_____
_____
_____

Today's Date: _____

What is your grief level from 0-10, with ten being the strongest? _____

What is your dominate feeling, emotion, or mood today? _____

What are your thoughts today?

_____
_____
_____
_____
_____
_____
_____
_____
_____
_____
_____
_____
_____
_____
_____
_____
_____
_____
_____
_____
_____
_____
_____
_____
_____
_____
_____
_____
_____
_____

Today's Date: _____

What is your grief level from 0-10, with ten being the strongest? _____

What is your dominate feeling, emotion, or mood today?
_____

What are your thoughts today?

_____
_____
_____
_____
_____
_____
_____
_____
_____
_____
_____
_____
_____
_____
_____
_____
_____
_____
_____
_____
_____
_____
_____
_____
_____
_____
_____
_____
_____

Today's Date: _____

What is your grief level from 0-10, with ten being the strongest? _____

What is your dominate feeling, emotion, or mood today? _____

What are your thoughts today?

_____

_____

_____

_____

_____

_____

_____

_____

_____

_____

_____

_____

_____

_____

_____

_____

_____

_____

_____

_____

_____

_____

_____

_____

_____

_____

_____

_____

Today's Date: _____

What is your grief level from 0-10, with ten being the strongest? _____

What is your dominate feeling, emotion, or mood today?
_____

What are your thoughts today?

_____
_____
_____
_____
_____
_____
_____
_____
_____
_____
_____
_____
_____
_____
_____
_____
_____
_____
_____
_____
_____
_____
_____
_____
_____
_____
_____
_____
_____
_____

Today's Date: _____

What is your grief level from 0-10, with ten being the strongest? _____

What is your dominate feeling, emotion, or mood today? _____

What are your thoughts today?

_____
_____
_____
_____
_____
_____
_____
_____
_____
_____
_____
_____
_____
_____
_____
_____
_____
_____
_____
_____
_____
_____
_____
_____
_____
_____
_____

Today's Date: _____

What is your grief level from 0-10, with ten being the strongest? _____

What is your dominate feeling, emotion, or mood today?
_____

What are your thoughts today?

_____
_____
_____
_____
_____
_____
_____
_____
_____
_____
_____
_____
_____
_____
_____
_____
_____
_____
_____
_____
_____
_____
_____
_____
_____
_____
_____
_____
_____
_____
_____

Today's Date: _____

What is your grief level from 0-10, with ten being the strongest? _____

What is your dominate feeling, emotion, or mood today? _____

What are your thoughts today?

_____
_____
_____
_____
_____
_____
_____
_____
_____
_____
_____
_____
_____
_____
_____
_____
_____
_____
_____
_____
_____
_____
_____
_____
_____
_____
_____
_____
_____

Today's Date: _____

What is your grief level from 0-10, with ten being the strongest? _____

What is your dominate feeling, emotion, or mood today?

_____

What are your thoughts today?

_____

_____

_____

_____

_____

_____

_____

_____

_____

_____

_____

_____

_____

_____

_____

_____

_____

_____

_____

_____

_____

_____

_____

_____

_____

_____

_____

_____

_____

Today's Date: _____

What is your grief level from 0-10, with ten being the
strongest? _____

What is your dominate feeling, emotion, or mood today?
_____

What are your thoughts today?

_____
_____
_____
_____
_____
_____
_____
_____
_____
_____
_____
_____
_____
_____
_____
_____
_____
_____
_____
_____
_____
_____
_____
_____
_____
_____
_____
_____
_____
_____

Tears are words that fall from the eyes.

~Lisa Mikell

Today's Date: _____

What is your grief level from 0-10, with ten being the strongest? _____

What is your dominate feeling, emotion, or mood today?
_____

What are your thoughts today?

_____
_____
_____
_____
_____
_____
_____
_____
_____
_____
_____
_____
_____
_____
_____
_____
_____
_____
_____
_____
_____
_____
_____
_____
_____
_____
_____
_____

Today's Date: _____

What is your grief level from 0-10, with ten being the strongest? _____

What is your dominate felling, emotion, or mood today?
_____

What are your thoughts today?

_____

_____

_____

_____

_____

_____

_____

_____

_____

_____

_____

_____

_____

_____

_____

_____

_____

_____

_____

_____

_____

_____

_____

_____

_____

_____

_____

_____

Today's Date: _____

What is your grief level from 0-10, with ten being the
strongest? _____

What is your dominate feeling, emotion, or mood today?
_____

What are your thoughts today?

_____
_____
_____
_____
_____
_____
_____
_____
_____
_____
_____
_____
_____
_____
_____
_____
_____
_____
_____
_____
_____
_____
_____
_____
_____
_____
_____
_____
_____

Today's Date: _____

What is your grief level from 0-10, with ten being the strongest? _____

What is your dominate felling, emotion, or mood today?
_____

What are your thoughts today?

_____
_____
_____
_____
_____
_____
_____
_____
_____
_____
_____
_____
_____
_____
_____
_____
_____
_____
_____
_____
_____
_____
_____
_____
_____
_____
_____
_____
_____

Today's Date: _____

What is your grief level from 0-10, with ten being the strongest? _____

What is your dominate feeling, emotion, or mood today?
_____

What are your thoughts today?

_____
_____
_____
_____
_____
_____
_____
_____
_____
_____
_____
_____
_____
_____
_____
_____
_____
_____
_____
_____
_____
_____
_____
_____
_____
_____
_____
_____

Today's Date: _____

What is your grief level from 0-10, with ten being the strongest? _____

What is your dominate felling, emotion, or mood today?
_____

What are your thoughts today?

_____
_____
_____
_____
_____
_____
_____
_____
_____
_____
_____
_____
_____
_____
_____
_____
_____
_____
_____
_____
_____
_____
_____
_____
_____
_____
_____
_____
_____

Today's Date: _____

What is your grief level from 0-10, with ten being the strongest? _____

What is your dominate feeling, emotion, or mood today? _____

What are your thoughts today?

_____
_____
_____
_____
_____
_____
_____
_____
_____
_____
_____
_____
_____
_____
_____
_____
_____
_____
_____
_____
_____
_____
_____
_____
_____
_____
_____
_____
_____

Today's Date: _____

What is your grief level from 0-10, with ten being the strongest? _____

What is your dominate felling, emotion, or mood today? _____

What are your thoughts today?

_____
_____
_____
_____
_____
_____
_____
_____
_____
_____
_____
_____
_____
_____
_____
_____
_____
_____
_____
_____
_____
_____
_____
_____
_____
_____
_____
_____
_____

Today's Date: _____

What is your grief level from 0-10, with ten being the strongest? _____

What is your dominate feeling, emotion, or mood today? _____

What are your thoughts today?

_____

_____

_____

_____

_____

_____

_____

_____

_____

_____

_____

_____

_____

_____

_____

_____

_____

_____

_____

_____

_____

_____

_____

_____

_____

_____

_____

_____

_____

Today's Date: _____

What is your grief level from 0-10, with ten being the strongest? _____

What is your dominate felling, emotion, or mood today? _____

What are your thoughts today?

_____
_____
_____
_____
_____
_____
_____
_____
_____
_____
_____
_____
_____
_____
_____
_____
_____
_____
_____
_____
_____
_____
_____
_____
_____
_____

Today's Date: _____

What is your grief level from 0-10, with ten being the strongest? _____

What is your dominate feeling, emotion, or mood today? _____

What are your thoughts today?

_____
_____
_____
_____
_____
_____
_____
_____
_____
_____
_____
_____
_____
_____
_____
_____
_____
_____
_____
_____
_____
_____
_____
_____
_____
_____
_____
_____
_____

Today's Date: _____

What is your grief level from 0-10, with ten being the
strongest? _____

What is your dominate feeling, emotion, or mood today?
_____

What are your thoughts today?

_____
_____
_____
_____
_____
_____
_____
_____
_____
_____
_____
_____
_____
_____
_____
_____
_____
_____
_____
_____
_____
_____
_____
_____
_____
_____
_____
_____
_____
_____

Today's Date: _____

What is your grief level from 0-10, with ten being the strongest? _____

What is your dominate feeling, emotion, or mood today? _____

What are your thoughts today?

_____
_____
_____
_____
_____
_____
_____
_____
_____
_____
_____
_____
_____
_____
_____
_____
_____
_____
_____
_____
_____
_____
_____
_____
_____
_____
_____
_____
_____

Today's Date: _____

What is your grief level from 0-10, with ten being the strongest? _____

What is your dominate feeling, emotion, or mood today?
_____

What are your thoughts today?

_____
_____
_____
_____
_____
_____
_____
_____
_____
_____
_____
_____
_____
_____
_____
_____
_____
_____
_____
_____
_____
_____
_____
_____
_____
_____
_____
_____
_____

Today's Date: _____

What is your grief level from 0-10, with ten being the strongest? _____

What is your dominate feeling, emotion, or mood today?
_____

What are your thoughts today?

_____
_____
_____
_____
_____
_____
_____
_____
_____
_____
_____
_____
_____
_____
_____
_____
_____
_____
_____
_____
_____
_____
_____
_____
_____
_____
_____
_____

Today's Date: _____

What is your grief level from 0-10, with ten being the strongest? _____

What is your dominate feeling, emotion, or mood today? _____

What are your thoughts today?

_____
_____
_____
_____
_____
_____
_____
_____
_____
_____
_____
_____
_____
_____
_____
_____
_____
_____
_____
_____
_____
_____
_____
_____
_____
_____
_____
_____
_____
_____

Today's Date: _____

What is your grief level from 0-10, with ten being the strongest? _____

What is your dominate feeling, emotion, or mood today?
_____

What are your thoughts today?

_____
_____
_____
_____
_____
_____
_____
_____
_____
_____
_____
_____
_____
_____
_____
_____
_____
_____
_____
_____
_____
_____
_____
_____
_____
_____
_____
_____
_____

Today's Date: _____

What is your grief level from 0-10, with ten being the strongest? _____

What is your dominate feeling, emotion, or mood today?
_____

What are your thoughts today?

_____
_____
_____
_____
_____
_____
_____
_____
_____
_____
_____
_____
_____
_____
_____
_____
_____
_____
_____
_____
_____
_____
_____
_____
_____
_____
_____
_____
_____
_____

Today's Date: _____

What is your grief level from 0-10, with ten being the strongest? _____

What is your dominate feeling, emotion, or mood today?
_____

What are your thoughts today?

_____
_____
_____
_____
_____
_____
_____
_____
_____
_____
_____
_____
_____
_____
_____
_____
_____
_____
_____
_____
_____
_____
_____
_____
_____
_____
_____
_____
_____

Today's Date: _____

What is your grief level from 0-10, with ten being the strongest? _____

What is your dominate feeling, emotion, or mood today?
_____

What are your thoughts today?

_____
_____
_____
_____
_____
_____
_____
_____
_____
_____
_____
_____
_____
_____
_____
_____
_____
_____
_____
_____
_____
_____
_____
_____
_____
_____
_____
_____
_____

Today's Date: _____

What is your grief level from 0-10, with ten being the
strongest? _____

What is your dominate feeling, emotion, or mood today?
_____

What are your thoughts today?

_____
_____
_____
_____
_____
_____
_____
_____
_____
_____
_____
_____
_____
_____
_____
_____
_____
_____
_____
_____
_____
_____
_____
_____
_____
_____
_____
_____
_____

Today's Date: _____

What is your grief level from 0-10, with ten being the strongest? _____

What is your dominate feeling, emotion, or mood today?
_____

What are your thoughts today?

_____
_____
_____
_____
_____
_____
_____
_____
_____
_____
_____
_____
_____
_____
_____
_____
_____
_____
_____
_____
_____
_____
_____
_____
_____
_____
_____
_____
_____

Today's Date: _____

What is your grief level from 0-10, with ten being the strongest? _____

What is your dominate feeling, emotion, or mood today?
_____

What are your thoughts today?

_____
_____
_____
_____
_____
_____
_____
_____
_____
_____
_____
_____
_____
_____
_____
_____
_____
_____
_____
_____
_____
_____
_____
_____
_____
_____

Today's Date: _____

What is your grief level from 0-10, with ten being the strongest? _____

What is your dominate feeling, emotion, or mood today?

_____

What are your thoughts today?

_____

_____

_____

_____

_____

_____

_____

_____

_____

_____

_____

_____

_____

_____

_____

_____

_____

_____

_____

_____

_____

_____

_____

_____

_____

_____

_____

_____

Today's Date: _____

What is your grief level from 0-10, with ten being the strongest? _____

What is your dominate feeling, emotion, or mood today?
_____

What are your thoughts today?

_____
_____
_____
_____
_____
_____
_____
_____
_____
_____
_____
_____
_____
_____
_____
_____
_____
_____
_____
_____
_____
_____
_____
_____
_____
_____
_____
_____

Today's Date: _____

What is your grief level from 0-10, with ten being the strongest? _____

What is your dominate feeling, emotion, or mood today?
_____

What are your thoughts today?

_____
_____
_____
_____
_____
_____
_____
_____
_____
_____
_____
_____
_____
_____
_____
_____
_____
_____
_____
_____
_____
_____
_____
_____
_____
_____
_____
_____

Today's Date: _____

What is your grief level from 0-10, with ten being the strongest? _____

What is your dominate feeling, emotion, or mood today?
_____

What are your thoughts today?

_____
_____
_____
_____
_____
_____
_____
_____
_____
_____
_____
_____
_____
_____
_____
_____
_____
_____
_____
_____
_____
_____
_____
_____
_____
_____
_____
_____

Today's Date: _____

What is your grief level from 0-10, with ten being the
strongest? _____

What is your dominate feeling, emotion, or mood today?

_____

What are your thoughts today?

_____

_____

_____

_____

_____

_____

_____

_____

_____

_____

_____

_____

_____

_____

_____

_____

_____

_____

_____

_____

_____

_____

_____

_____

_____

_____

_____

_____

_____

Today's Date: _____

What is your grief level from 0-10, with ten being the strongest? _____

What is your dominate feeling, emotion, or mood today?
_____

What are your thoughts today?

_____
_____
_____
_____
_____
_____
_____
_____
_____
_____
_____
_____
_____
_____
_____
_____
_____
_____
_____
_____
_____
_____
_____
_____
_____
_____
_____
_____
_____
_____

Today's Date: _____

What is your grief level from 0-10, with ten being the strongest? _____

What is your dominate feeling, emotion, or mood today? _____

What are your thoughts today?

_____
_____
_____
_____
_____
_____
_____
_____
_____
_____
_____
_____
_____
_____
_____
_____
_____
_____
_____
_____
_____
_____
_____
_____
_____
_____
_____
_____
_____
_____

Today's Date: _____

What is your grief level from 0-10, with ten being the strongest? _____

What is your dominate feeling, emotion, or mood today? _____

What are your thoughts today?

_____
_____
_____
_____
_____
_____
_____
_____
_____
_____
_____
_____
_____
_____
_____
_____
_____
_____
_____
_____
_____
_____
_____
_____
_____
_____
_____
_____

Romans 8:18 For I reckon that the sufferings of this present time are not worthy to be compared with the glory which shall be revealed in us.

~KJV

Today's Date: _____

What is your grief level from 0-10, with ten being the
strongest? _____

What is your dominate feeling, emotion, or mood today?
_____

What are your thoughts today?

_____
_____
_____
_____
_____
_____
_____
_____
_____
_____
_____
_____
_____
_____
_____
_____
_____
_____
_____
_____
_____
_____
_____
_____
_____
_____
_____
_____

Today's Date: _____

What is your grief level from 0-10, with ten being the
strongest? _____

What is your dominate felling, emotion, or mood today?
_____

What are your thoughts today?

_____
_____
_____
_____
_____
_____
_____
_____
_____
_____
_____
_____
_____
_____
_____
_____
_____
_____
_____
_____
_____
_____
_____
_____
_____
_____

Today's Date: _____

What is your grief level from 0-10, with ten being the strongest? _____

What is your dominate feeling, emotion, or mood today?
_____

What are your thoughts today?

_____
_____
_____
_____
_____
_____
_____
_____
_____
_____
_____
_____
_____
_____
_____
_____
_____
_____
_____
_____
_____
_____
_____
_____
_____
_____
_____
_____
_____
_____
_____

Today's Date: _____

What is your grief level from 0-10, with ten being the strongest? _____

What is your dominate felling, emotion, or mood today?
_____

What are your thoughts today?

_____
_____
_____
_____
_____
_____
_____
_____
_____
_____
_____
_____
_____
_____
_____
_____
_____
_____
_____
_____
_____
_____
_____
_____
_____
_____
_____
_____

Today's Date: _____

What is your grief level from 0-10, with ten being the strongest? _____

What is your dominate feeling, emotion, or mood today?
_____

What are your thoughts today?

_____
_____
_____
_____
_____
_____
_____
_____
_____
_____
_____
_____
_____
_____
_____
_____
_____
_____
_____
_____
_____
_____
_____
_____
_____
_____
_____
_____
_____

Today's Date: _____

What is your grief level from 0-10, with ten being the
strongest? _____

What is your dominate felling, emotion, or mood today?
_____

What are your thoughts today?

_____
_____
_____
_____
_____
_____
_____
_____
_____
_____
_____
_____
_____
_____
_____
_____
_____
_____
_____
_____
_____
_____
_____
_____
_____
_____
_____
_____
_____
_____

Today's Date: _____

What is your grief level from 0-10, with ten being the strongest? _____

What is your dominate feeling, emotion, or mood today?
_____

What are your thoughts today?

_____
_____
_____
_____
_____
_____
_____
_____
_____
_____
_____
_____
_____
_____
_____
_____
_____
_____
_____
_____
_____
_____
_____
_____
_____
_____
_____
_____

Today's Date: _____

What is your grief level from 0-10, with ten being the strongest? _____

What is your dominate felling, emotion, or mood today?
_____

What are your thoughts today?

_____
_____
_____
_____
_____
_____
_____
_____
_____
_____
_____
_____
_____
_____
_____
_____
_____
_____
_____
_____
_____
_____
_____
_____
_____
_____
_____
_____
_____
_____

Today's Date: _____

What is your grief level from 0-10, with ten being the strongest? _____

What is your dominate feeling, emotion, or mood today? _____

What are your thoughts today?

_____
_____
_____
_____
_____
_____
_____
_____
_____
_____
_____
_____
_____
_____
_____
_____
_____
_____
_____
_____
_____
_____
_____
_____
_____
_____
_____

Today's Date: _____

What is your grief level from 0-10, with ten being the strongest? _____

What is your dominate felling, emotion, or mood today?
_____

What are your thoughts today?

_____

_____

_____

_____

_____

_____

_____

_____

_____

_____

_____

_____

_____

_____

_____

_____

_____

_____

_____

_____

_____

_____

_____

_____

_____

_____

_____

Today's Date: _____

What is your grief level from 0-10, with ten being the
strongest? _____

What is your dominate feeling, emotion, or mood today?
_____

What are your thoughts today?

_____
_____
_____
_____
_____
_____
_____
_____
_____
_____
_____
_____
_____
_____
_____
_____
_____
_____
_____
_____
_____
_____
_____
_____
_____
_____
_____
_____
_____

Today's Date: _____

What is your grief level from 0-10, with ten being the
strongest? _____

What is your dominate feeling, emotion, or mood today?
_____

What are your thoughts today?

_____
_____
_____
_____
_____
_____
_____
_____
_____
_____
_____
_____
_____
_____
_____
_____
_____
_____
_____
_____
_____
_____
_____
_____
_____
_____
_____
_____
_____
_____

Today's Date: _____

What is your grief level from 0-10, with ten being the strongest? _____

What is your dominate feeling, emotion, or mood today? _____

What are your thoughts today?

_____
_____
_____
_____
_____
_____
_____
_____
_____
_____
_____
_____
_____
_____
_____
_____
_____
_____
_____
_____
_____
_____
_____
_____
_____
_____
_____
_____

Today's Date: _____

What is your grief level from 0-10, with ten being the strongest? _____

What is your dominate feeling, emotion, or mood today?
_____

What are your thoughts today?

_____
_____
_____
_____
_____
_____
_____
_____
_____
_____
_____
_____
_____
_____
_____
_____
_____
_____
_____
_____
_____
_____
_____
_____
_____
_____
_____
_____

Today's Date: _____

What is your grief level from 0-10, with ten being the
strongest? _____

What is your dominate feeling, emotion, or mood today?
_____

What are your thoughts today?

_____
_____
_____
_____
_____
_____
_____
_____
_____
_____
_____
_____
_____
_____
_____
_____
_____
_____
_____
_____
_____
_____
_____
_____
_____
_____
_____
_____
_____

Today's Date: _____

What is your grief level from 0-10, with ten being the
strongest? _____

What is your dominate feeling, emotion, or mood today?
_____

What are your thoughts today?

_____
_____
_____
_____
_____
_____
_____
_____
_____
_____
_____
_____
_____
_____
_____
_____
_____
_____
_____
_____
_____
_____
_____
_____
_____
_____
_____
_____
_____

Today's Date: _____

What is your grief level from 0-10, with ten being the
strongest? _____

What is your dominate feeling, emotion, or mood today?
_____

What are your thoughts today?

_____
_____
_____
_____
_____
_____
_____
_____
_____
_____
_____
_____
_____
_____
_____
_____
_____
_____
_____
_____
_____
_____
_____
_____
_____
_____
_____
_____

Today's Date: _____

What is your grief level from 0-10, with ten being the strongest? _____

What is your dominate feeling, emotion, or mood today?

_____

What are your thoughts today?

_____

_____

_____

_____

_____

_____

_____

_____

_____

_____

_____

_____

_____

_____

_____

_____

_____

_____

_____

_____

_____

_____

_____

_____

_____

_____

_____

_____

_____

_____

Today's Date: _____

What is your grief level from 0-10, with ten being the strongest? _____

What is your dominate feeling, emotion, or mood today?
_____

What are your thoughts today?

_____
_____
_____
_____
_____
_____
_____
_____
_____
_____
_____
_____
_____
_____
_____
_____
_____
_____
_____
_____
_____
_____
_____
_____
_____
_____
_____
_____
_____
_____

Today's Date: _____

What is your grief level from 0-10, with ten being the strongest? _____

What is your dominate feeling, emotion, or mood today? _____

What are your thoughts today?

_____
_____
_____
_____
_____
_____
_____
_____
_____
_____
_____
_____
_____
_____
_____
_____
_____
_____
_____
_____
_____
_____
_____
_____
_____
_____
_____
_____

Today's Date: _____

What is your grief level from 0-10, with ten being the strongest? _____

What is your dominate feeling, emotion, or mood today?
_____

What are your thoughts today?

_____

_____

_____

_____

_____

_____

_____

_____

_____

_____

_____

_____

_____

_____

_____

_____

_____

_____

_____

_____

_____

_____

_____

_____

_____

_____

_____

_____

Today's Date: _____

What is your grief level from 0-10, with ten being the
strongest? _____

What is your dominate feeling, emotion, or mood today?

_____

What are your thoughts today?

_____

_____

_____

_____

_____

_____

_____

_____

_____

_____

_____

_____

_____

_____

_____

_____

_____

_____

_____

_____

_____

_____

_____

_____

_____

_____

_____

_____

_____

Today's Date: _____

What is your grief level from 0-10, with ten being the strongest? _____

What is your dominate feeling, emotion, or mood today?
_____

What are your thoughts today?

_____
_____
_____
_____
_____
_____
_____
_____
_____
_____
_____
_____
_____
_____
_____
_____
_____
_____
_____
_____
_____
_____
_____
_____
_____
_____
_____
_____
_____

Today's Date: _____

What is your grief level from 0-10, with ten being the strongest? _____

What is your dominate feeling, emotion, or mood today?
_____

What are your thoughts today?

_____
_____
_____
_____
_____
_____
_____
_____
_____
_____
_____
_____
_____
_____
_____
_____
_____
_____
_____
_____
_____
_____
_____
_____
_____
_____
_____
_____

Today's Date: _____

What is your grief level from 0-10, with ten being the strongest? _____

What is your dominate feeling, emotion, or mood today?
_____

What are your thoughts today?

_____
_____
_____
_____
_____
_____
_____
_____
_____
_____
_____
_____
_____
_____
_____
_____
_____
_____
_____
_____
_____
_____
_____
_____
_____
_____
_____
_____
_____

Today's Date: _____

What is your grief level from 0-10, with ten being the strongest? _____

What is your dominate feeling, emotion, or mood today?
_____

What are your thoughts today?

_____
_____
_____
_____
_____
_____
_____
_____
_____
_____
_____
_____
_____
_____
_____
_____
_____
_____
_____
_____
_____
_____
_____
_____
_____
_____
_____
_____
_____

Today's Date: _____

What is your grief level from 0-10, with ten being the strongest? _____

What is your dominate feeling, emotion, or mood today? _____

What are your thoughts today?

_____
_____
_____
_____
_____
_____
_____
_____
_____
_____
_____
_____
_____
_____
_____
_____
_____
_____
_____
_____
_____
_____
_____
_____
_____
_____
_____
_____
_____
_____

Today's Date: _____

What is your grief level from 0-10, with ten being the
strongest? _____

What is your dominate feeling, emotion, or mood today?
_____

What are your thoughts today?

_____

_____

_____

_____

_____

_____

_____

_____

_____

_____

_____

_____

_____

_____

_____

_____

_____

_____

_____

_____

_____

_____

_____

_____

_____

_____

_____

_____

_____

_____

Today's Date: _____

What is your grief level from 0-10, with ten being the strongest? _____

What is your dominate feeling, emotion, or mood today? _____

What are your thoughts today?

_____
_____
_____
_____
_____
_____
_____
_____
_____
_____
_____
_____
_____
_____
_____
_____
_____
_____
_____
_____
_____
_____
_____
_____
_____
_____
_____
_____
_____

Today's Date: _____

What is your grief level from 0-10, with ten being the strongest? _____

What is your dominate feeling, emotion, or mood today?
_____

What are your thoughts today?

_____
_____
_____
_____
_____
_____
_____
_____
_____
_____
_____
_____
_____
_____
_____
_____
_____
_____
_____
_____
_____
_____
_____
_____
_____
_____
_____
_____
_____

Today's Date: _____

What is your grief level from 0-10, with ten being the strongest? _____

What is your dominate feeling, emotion, or mood today? _____

What are your thoughts today?

_____
_____
_____
_____
_____
_____
_____
_____
_____
_____
_____
_____
_____
_____
_____
_____
_____
_____
_____
_____
_____
_____
_____
_____
_____
_____
_____
_____

With all that He has to do,
He still gets back to you.

~D. K.

Today's Date: _____

What is your grief level from 0-10, with ten being the strongest? _____

What is your dominate feeling, emotion, or mood today?
_____

What are your thoughts today?

_____
_____
_____
_____
_____
_____
_____
_____
_____
_____
_____
_____
_____
_____
_____
_____
_____
_____
_____
_____
_____
_____
_____
_____
_____
_____
_____
_____

Today's Date: _____

What is your grief level from 0-10, with ten being the strongest? _____

What is your dominate felling, emotion, or mood today?
_____

What are your thoughts today?

_____
_____
_____
_____
_____
_____
_____
_____
_____
_____
_____
_____
_____
_____
_____
_____
_____
_____
_____
_____
_____
_____
_____
_____
_____
_____
_____
_____
_____
_____

Today's Date: _____

What is your grief level from 0-10, with ten being the strongest? _____

What is your dominate feeling, emotion, or mood today?
_____

What are your thoughts today?

_____
_____
_____
_____
_____
_____
_____
_____
_____
_____
_____
_____
_____
_____
_____
_____
_____
_____
_____
_____
_____
_____
_____
_____
_____
_____
_____
_____

Today's Date: _____

What is your grief level from 0-10, with ten being the strongest? _____

What is your dominate felling, emotion, or mood today?
_____

What are your thoughts today?

_____
_____
_____
_____
_____
_____
_____
_____
_____
_____
_____
_____
_____
_____
_____
_____
_____
_____
_____
_____
_____
_____
_____
_____
_____
_____
_____
_____
_____
_____
_____

Today's Date: _____

What is your grief level from 0-10, with ten being the strongest? _____

What is your dominate feeling, emotion, or mood today?
_____

What are your thoughts today?

_____
_____
_____
_____
_____
_____
_____
_____
_____
_____
_____
_____
_____
_____
_____
_____
_____
_____
_____
_____
_____
_____
_____
_____
_____
_____
_____
_____

Today's Date: _____

What is your grief level from 0-10, with ten being the strongest? _____

What is your dominate felling, emotion, or mood today?

_____

What are your thoughts today?

_____

_____

_____

_____

_____

_____

_____

_____

_____

_____

_____

_____

_____

_____

_____

_____

_____

_____

_____

_____

_____

_____

_____

_____

_____

_____

_____

_____

Today's Date: _____

What is your grief level from 0-10, with ten being the strongest? _____

What is your dominate feeling, emotion, or mood today?
_____

What are your thoughts today?

_____
_____
_____
_____
_____
_____
_____
_____
_____
_____
_____
_____
_____
_____
_____
_____
_____
_____
_____
_____
_____
_____
_____
_____
_____
_____
_____
_____

Today's Date: _____

What is your grief level from 0-10, with ten being the strongest? _____

What is your dominate felling, emotion, or mood today?
_____

What are your thoughts today?

_____

_____

_____

_____

_____

_____

_____

_____

_____

_____

_____

_____

_____

_____

_____

_____

_____

_____

_____

_____

_____

_____

_____

_____

_____

_____

_____

_____

Today's Date: _____

What is your grief level from 0-10, with ten being the strongest? _____

What is your dominate feeling, emotion, or mood today?
_____

What are your thoughts today?

_____
_____
_____
_____
_____
_____
_____
_____
_____
_____
_____
_____
_____
_____
_____
_____
_____
_____
_____
_____
_____
_____
_____
_____
_____
_____
_____
_____
_____
_____

Today's Date: _____

What is your grief level from 0-10, with ten being the strongest? _____

What is your dominate felling, emotion, or mood today? _____

What are your thoughts today?

_____
_____
_____
_____
_____
_____
_____
_____
_____
_____
_____
_____
_____
_____
_____
_____
_____
_____
_____
_____
_____
_____
_____
_____
_____
_____
_____
_____

Today's Date: _____

What is your grief level from 0-10, with ten being the strongest? _____

What is your dominate feeling, emotion, or mood today? _____

What are your thoughts today?

_____
_____
_____
_____
_____
_____
_____
_____
_____
_____
_____
_____
_____
_____
_____
_____
_____
_____
_____
_____
_____
_____
_____
_____
_____
_____

Today's Date: _____

What is your grief level from 0-10, with ten being the strongest? _____

What is your dominate feeling, emotion, or mood today? _____

What are your thoughts today?

_____
_____
_____
_____
_____
_____
_____
_____
_____
_____
_____
_____
_____
_____
_____
_____
_____
_____
_____
_____
_____
_____
_____
_____
_____
_____
_____
_____

Today's Date: _____

What is your grief level from 0-10, with ten being the strongest? _____

What is your dominate feeling, emotion, or mood today? _____

What are your thoughts today?

_____
_____
_____
_____
_____
_____
_____
_____
_____
_____
_____
_____
_____
_____
_____
_____
_____
_____
_____
_____
_____
_____
_____
_____
_____
_____
_____
_____
_____

Today's Date: _____

What is your grief level from 0-10, with ten being the
strongest? _____

What is your dominate feeling, emotion, or mood today?
_____

What are your thoughts today?

_____
_____
_____
_____
_____
_____
_____
_____
_____
_____
_____
_____
_____
_____
_____
_____
_____
_____
_____
_____
_____
_____
_____
_____
_____
_____
_____
_____
_____
_____
_____

Today's Date: _____

What is your grief level from 0-10, with ten being the strongest? _____

What is your dominate feeling, emotion, or mood today?
_____

What are your thoughts today?

_____

_____

_____

_____

_____

_____

_____

_____

_____

_____

_____

_____

_____

_____

_____

_____

_____

_____

_____

_____

_____

_____

_____

_____

_____

_____

_____

_____

Today's Date: _____

What is your grief level from 0-10, with ten being the
strongest? _____

What is your dominate feeling, emotion, or mood today?
_____

What are your thoughts today?

_____
_____
_____
_____
_____
_____
_____
_____
_____
_____
_____
_____
_____
_____
_____
_____
_____
_____
_____
_____
_____
_____
_____
_____
_____
_____
_____
_____

Today's Date: _____

What is your grief level from 0-10, with ten being the strongest? _____

What is your dominate feeling, emotion, or mood today? _____

What are your thoughts today?

_____
_____
_____
_____
_____
_____
_____
_____
_____
_____
_____
_____
_____
_____
_____
_____
_____
_____
_____
_____
_____
_____
_____
_____
_____
_____
_____
_____

Today's Date: _____

What is your grief level from 0-10, with ten being the strongest? _____

What is your dominate feeling, emotion, or mood today?
_____

What are your thoughts today?

_____
_____
_____
_____
_____
_____
_____
_____
_____
_____
_____
_____
_____
_____
_____
_____
_____
_____
_____
_____
_____
_____
_____
_____
_____
_____
_____
_____
_____

Today's Date: _____

What is your grief level from 0-10, with ten being the strongest? _____

What is your dominate feeling, emotion, or mood today? _____

What are your thoughts today?

_____
_____
_____
_____
_____
_____
_____
_____
_____
_____
_____
_____
_____
_____
_____
_____
_____
_____
_____
_____
_____
_____
_____
_____
_____
_____
_____
_____

Today's Date: _____

What is your grief level from 0-10, with ten being the strongest? _____

What is your dominate feeling, emotion, or mood today?
_____

What are your thoughts today?

_____

_____

_____

_____

_____

_____

_____

_____

_____

_____

_____

_____

_____

_____

_____

_____

_____

_____

_____

_____

_____

_____

_____

_____

_____

_____

_____

_____

Today's Date: _____

What is your grief level from 0-10, with ten being the strongest? _____

What is your dominate feeling, emotion, or mood today? _____

What are your thoughts today?

_____
_____
_____
_____
_____
_____
_____
_____
_____
_____
_____
_____
_____
_____
_____
_____
_____
_____
_____
_____
_____
_____
_____
_____
_____
_____
_____

Today's Date: _____

What is your grief level from 0-10, with ten being the strongest? _____

What is your dominate feeling, emotion, or mood today?
_____

What are your thoughts today?

_____
_____
_____
_____
_____
_____
_____
_____
_____
_____
_____
_____
_____
_____
_____
_____
_____
_____
_____
_____
_____
_____
_____
_____
_____
_____
_____
_____
_____

Today's Date: _____

What is your grief level from 0-10, with ten being the strongest? _____

What is your dominate feeling, emotion, or mood today?
_____

What are your thoughts today?

_____
_____
_____
_____
_____
_____
_____
_____
_____
_____
_____
_____
_____
_____
_____
_____
_____
_____
_____
_____
_____
_____
_____
_____
_____
_____
_____
_____
_____
_____

Today's Date: _____

What is your grief level from 0-10, with ten being the strongest? _____

What is your dominate feeling, emotion, or mood today?
_____

What are your thoughts today?

_____
_____
_____
_____
_____
_____
_____
_____
_____
_____
_____
_____
_____
_____
_____
_____
_____
_____
_____
_____
_____
_____
_____
_____
_____
_____
_____
_____
_____

Today's Date: _____

What is your grief level from 0-10, with ten being the strongest? _____

What is your dominate feeling, emotion, or mood today?
_____

What are your thoughts today?

_____
_____
_____
_____
_____
_____
_____
_____
_____
_____
_____
_____
_____
_____
_____
_____
_____
_____
_____
_____
_____
_____
_____
_____
_____
_____
_____
_____
_____

Today's Date: _____

What is your grief level from 0-10, with ten being the strongest? _____

What is your dominate feeling, emotion, or mood today?
_____

What are your thoughts today?

_____
_____
_____
_____
_____
_____
_____
_____
_____
_____
_____
_____
_____
_____
_____
_____
_____
_____
_____
_____
_____
_____
_____
_____
_____
_____
_____

Today's Date: _____

What is your grief level from 0-10, with ten being the strongest? _____

What is your dominate feeling, emotion, or mood today?
_____

What are your thoughts today?

_____
_____
_____
_____
_____
_____
_____
_____
_____
_____
_____
_____
_____
_____
_____
_____
_____
_____
_____
_____
_____
_____
_____
_____
_____
_____
_____
_____

Today's Date: _____

What is your grief level from 0-10, with ten being the
strongest? _____

What is your dominate feeling, emotion, or mood today?
_____

What are your thoughts today?

_____
_____
_____
_____
_____
_____
_____
_____
_____
_____
_____
_____
_____
_____
_____
_____
_____
_____
_____
_____
_____
_____
_____
_____
_____
_____
_____
_____
_____
_____

Today's Date: _____

What is your grief level from 0-10, with ten being the strongest? _____

What is your dominate feeling, emotion, or mood today? _____

What are your thoughts today?

_____
_____
_____
_____
_____
_____
_____
_____
_____
_____
_____
_____
_____
_____
_____
_____
_____
_____
_____
_____
_____
_____
_____
_____
_____
_____

Today's Date: _____

What is your grief level from 0-10, with ten being the strongest? _____

What is your dominate feeling, emotion, or mood today?
_____

What are your thoughts today?

_____
_____
_____
_____
_____
_____
_____
_____
_____
_____
_____
_____
_____
_____
_____
_____
_____
_____
_____
_____
_____
_____
_____
_____
_____
_____
_____
_____
_____
_____
_____
_____

Today's Date: _____

What is your grief level from 0-10, with ten being the strongest? _____

What is your dominate feeling, emotion, or mood today?
_____

What are your thoughts today?

_____
_____
_____
_____
_____
_____
_____
_____
_____
_____
_____
_____
_____
_____
_____
_____
_____
_____
_____
_____
_____
_____
_____
_____
_____
_____
_____
_____
_____
_____

Philippians 4:13 I can do all things through Christ which strengtheneth me.

~KJV

Today's Date: _____

What is your grief level from 0-10, with ten being the strongest? _____

What is your dominate feeling, emotion, or mood today? _____

What are your thoughts today?

_____
_____
_____
_____
_____
_____
_____
_____
_____
_____
_____
_____
_____
_____
_____
_____
_____
_____
_____
_____
_____
_____
_____
_____
_____
_____
_____
_____

Today's Date: _____

What is your grief level from 0-10, with ten being the strongest? _____

What is your dominate felling, emotion, or mood today? _____

What are your thoughts today?

_____
_____
_____
_____
_____
_____
_____
_____
_____
_____
_____
_____
_____
_____
_____
_____
_____
_____
_____
_____
_____
_____
_____
_____
_____
_____
_____
_____

Today's Date: _____

What is your grief level from 0-10, with ten being the strongest? _____

What is your dominate feeling, emotion, or mood today? _____

What are your thoughts today?

_____

_____

_____

_____

_____

_____

_____

_____

_____

_____

_____

_____

_____

_____

_____

_____

_____

_____

_____

_____

_____

_____

_____

_____

_____

_____

_____

_____

_____

Today's Date: _____

What is your grief level from 0-10, with ten being the strongest? _____

What is your dominate felling, emotion, or mood today? _____

What are your thoughts today?

_____

_____

_____

_____

_____

_____

_____

_____

_____

_____

_____

_____

_____

_____

_____

_____

_____

_____

_____

_____

_____

_____

_____

_____

_____

_____

Today's Date: _____

What is your grief level from 0-10, with ten being the strongest? _____

What is your dominate feeling, emotion, or mood today? _____

What are your thoughts today?

_____

_____

_____

_____

_____

_____

_____

_____

_____

_____

_____

_____

_____

_____

_____

_____

_____

_____

_____

_____

_____

_____

_____

_____

_____

_____

_____

_____

Today's Date: _____

What is your grief level from 0-10, with ten being the strongest? _____

What is your dominate felling, emotion, or mood today?
_____

What are your thoughts today?

_____
_____
_____
_____
_____
_____
_____
_____
_____
_____
_____
_____
_____
_____
_____
_____
_____
_____
_____
_____
_____
_____
_____
_____
_____
_____

Today's Date: _____

What is your grief level from 0-10, with ten being the strongest? _____

What is your dominate feeling, emotion, or mood today? _____

What are your thoughts today?

_____
_____
_____
_____
_____
_____
_____
_____
_____
_____
_____
_____
_____
_____
_____
_____
_____
_____
_____
_____
_____
_____
_____
_____
_____
_____
_____
_____

Today's Date: _____

What is your grief level from 0-10, with ten being the strongest? _____

What is your dominate felling, emotion, or mood today?
_____

What are your thoughts today?

_____
_____
_____
_____
_____
_____
_____
_____
_____
_____
_____
_____
_____
_____
_____
_____
_____
_____
_____
_____
_____
_____
_____
_____
_____
_____

Today's Date: _____

What is your grief level from 0-10, with ten being the strongest? _____

What is your dominate feeling, emotion, or mood today? _____

What are your thoughts today?

_____

_____

_____

_____

_____

_____

_____

_____

_____

_____

_____

_____

_____

_____

_____

_____

_____

_____

_____

_____

_____

_____

_____

_____

_____

_____

_____

_____

Today's Date: _____

What is your grief level from 0-10, with ten being the strongest? _____

What is your dominate felling, emotion, or mood today?
_____

What are your thoughts today?

_____
_____
_____
_____
_____
_____
_____
_____
_____
_____
_____
_____
_____
_____
_____
_____
_____
_____
_____
_____
_____
_____
_____
_____
_____

Today's Date: _____

What is your grief level from 0-10, with ten being the strongest? _____

What is your dominate feeling, emotion, or mood today? _____

What are your thoughts today?

_____

_____

_____

_____

_____

_____

_____

_____

_____

_____

_____

_____

_____

_____

_____

_____

_____

_____

_____

_____

_____

_____

_____

_____

_____

Today's Date: _____

What is your grief level from 0-10, with ten being the strongest? _____

What is your dominate feeling, emotion, or mood today?
_____

What are your thoughts today?

_____
_____
_____
_____
_____
_____
_____
_____
_____
_____
_____
_____
_____
_____
_____
_____
_____
_____
_____
_____
_____
_____
_____
_____
_____
_____
_____
_____
_____

Today's Date: _____

What is your grief level from 0-10, with ten being the strongest? _____

What is your dominate feeling, emotion, or mood today? _____

What are your thoughts today?

_____

_____

_____

_____

_____

_____

_____

_____

_____

_____

_____

_____

_____

_____

_____

_____

_____

_____

_____

_____

_____

_____

_____

_____

Today's Date: _____

What is your grief level from 0-10, with ten being the strongest? _____

What is your dominate feeling, emotion, or mood today? _____

What are your thoughts today?

_____
_____
_____
_____
_____
_____
_____
_____
_____
_____
_____
_____
_____
_____
_____
_____
_____
_____
_____
_____
_____
_____
_____
_____
_____

Today's Date: _____

What is your grief level from 0-10, with ten being the strongest? _____

What is your dominate feeling, emotion, or mood today? _____

What are your thoughts today?

_____
_____
_____
_____
_____
_____
_____
_____
_____
_____
_____
_____
_____
_____
_____
_____
_____
_____
_____
_____
_____
_____
_____
_____
_____
_____
_____

Today's Date: _____

What is your grief level from 0-10, with ten being the strongest? _____

What is your dominate feeling, emotion, or mood today?
_____

What are your thoughts today?

_____
_____
_____
_____
_____
_____
_____
_____
_____
_____
_____
_____
_____
_____
_____
_____
_____
_____
_____
_____
_____
_____
_____
_____
_____
_____
_____
_____

Today's Date: _____

What is your grief level from 0-10, with ten being the strongest? _____

What is your dominate feeling, emotion, or mood today?
_____

What are your thoughts today?

_____
_____
_____
_____
_____
_____
_____
_____
_____
_____
_____
_____
_____
_____
_____
_____
_____
_____
_____
_____
_____
_____
_____
_____
_____
_____
_____
_____

Today's Date: _____

What is your grief level from 0-10, with ten being the strongest? _____

What is your dominate feeling, emotion, or mood today? _____

What are your thoughts today?

_____
_____
_____
_____
_____
_____
_____
_____
_____
_____
_____
_____
_____
_____
_____
_____
_____
_____
_____
_____
_____
_____
_____
_____
_____
_____
_____
_____

Today's Date: _____

What is your grief level from 0-10, with ten being the
strongest? _____

What is your dominate feeling, emotion, or mood today?
_____

What are your thoughts today?

_____
_____
_____
_____
_____
_____
_____
_____
_____
_____
_____
_____
_____
_____
_____
_____
_____
_____
_____
_____
_____
_____
_____
_____
_____
_____
_____
_____

Today's Date: _____

What is your grief level from 0-10, with ten being the strongest? _____

What is your dominate feeling, emotion, or mood today?
_____

What are your thoughts today?

_____
_____
_____
_____
_____
_____
_____
_____
_____
_____
_____
_____
_____
_____
_____
_____
_____
_____
_____
_____
_____
_____
_____
_____
_____
_____
_____
_____

Today's Date: _____

What is your grief level from 0-10, with ten being the strongest? _____

What is your dominate feeling, emotion, or mood today? _____

What are your thoughts today?

_____
_____
_____
_____
_____
_____
_____
_____
_____
_____
_____
_____
_____
_____
_____
_____
_____
_____
_____
_____
_____
_____
_____
_____
_____
_____
_____

Today's Date: _____

What is your grief level from 0-10, with ten being the strongest? _____

What is your dominate feeling, emotion, or mood today? _____

What are your thoughts today?

_____
_____
_____
_____
_____
_____
_____
_____
_____
_____
_____
_____
_____
_____
_____
_____
_____
_____
_____
_____
_____
_____
_____
_____
_____
_____
_____
_____

Today's Date: _____

What is your grief level from 0-10, with ten being the strongest? _____

What is your dominate feeling, emotion, or mood today? _____

What are your thoughts today?

_____

_____

_____

_____

_____

_____

_____

_____

_____

_____

_____

_____

_____

_____

_____

_____

_____

_____

_____

_____

_____

_____

_____

_____

_____

_____

_____

_____

Today's Date: _____

What is your grief level from 0-10, with ten being the strongest? _____

What is your dominate feeling, emotion, or mood today?
_____

What are your thoughts today?

_____
_____
_____
_____
_____
_____
_____
_____
_____
_____
_____
_____
_____
_____
_____
_____
_____
_____
_____
_____
_____
_____
_____
_____
_____
_____
_____
_____

Today's Date: _____

What is your grief level from 0-10, with ten being the strongest? _____

What is your dominate feeling, emotion, or mood today?
_____

What are your thoughts today?

_____
_____
_____
_____
_____
_____
_____
_____
_____
_____
_____
_____
_____
_____
_____
_____
_____
_____
_____
_____
_____
_____
_____
_____
_____
_____
_____
_____

Today's Date: _____

What is your grief level from 0-10, with ten being the strongest? _____

What is your dominate feeling, emotion, or mood today? _____

What are your thoughts today?

_____
_____
_____
_____
_____
_____
_____
_____
_____
_____
_____
_____
_____
_____
_____
_____
_____
_____
_____
_____
_____
_____
_____
_____
_____
_____
_____
_____

Today's Date: _____

What is your grief level from 0-10, with ten being the strongest? _____

What is your dominate feeling, emotion, or mood today? _____

What are your thoughts today?

_____

_____

_____

_____

_____

_____

_____

_____

_____

_____

_____

_____

_____

_____

_____

_____

_____

_____

_____

_____

_____

_____

_____

_____

_____

_____

_____

Today's Date: _____

What is your grief level from 0-10, with ten being the strongest? _____

What is your dominate feeling, emotion, or mood today? _____

What are your thoughts today?

_____
_____
_____
_____
_____
_____
_____
_____
_____
_____
_____
_____
_____
_____
_____
_____
_____
_____
_____
_____
_____
_____
_____
_____
_____
_____

Today's Date: _____

What is your grief level from 0-10, with ten being the
strongest? _____

What is your dominate feeling, emotion, or mood today?
_____

What are your thoughts today?

_____

_____

_____

_____

_____

_____

_____

_____

_____

_____

_____

_____

_____

_____

_____

_____

_____

_____

_____

_____

_____

_____

_____

_____

_____

_____

_____

_____

Today's Date: _____

What is your grief level from 0-10, with ten being the strongest? _____

What is your dominate feeling, emotion, or mood today? _____

What are your thoughts today?

_____
_____
_____
_____
_____
_____
_____
_____
_____
_____
_____
_____
_____
_____
_____
_____
_____
_____
_____
_____
_____
_____
_____
_____
_____
_____
_____
_____

Today's Date: _____

What is your grief level from 0-10, with ten being the strongest? _____

What is your dominate feeling, emotion, or mood today? _____

What are your thoughts today?

_____
_____
_____
_____
_____
_____
_____
_____
_____
_____
_____
_____
_____
_____
_____
_____
_____
_____
_____
_____
_____
_____
_____
_____
_____
_____
_____
_____
_____

Psalm 119.28 My soul melteth for heaviness. Strengthen thou me according unto thy word.

~KJV

Today's Date: _____

What is your grief level from 0-10, with ten being the strongest? _____

What is your dominate feeling, emotion, or mood today?
_____

What are your thoughts today?

_____
_____
_____
_____
_____
_____
_____
_____
_____
_____
_____
_____
_____
_____
_____
_____
_____
_____
_____
_____
_____
_____
_____
_____
_____
_____
_____
_____

Today's Date: _____

What is your grief level from 0-10, with ten being the
strongest? _____

What is your dominate felling, emotion, or mood today?
_____

What are your thoughts today?

_____

_____

_____

_____

_____

_____

_____

_____

_____

_____

_____

_____

_____

_____

_____

_____

_____

_____

_____

_____

_____

_____

_____

_____

_____

_____

_____

_____

Today's Date: _____

What is your grief level from 0-10, with ten being the strongest? _____

What is your dominate feeling, emotion, or mood today? _____

What are your thoughts today?

_____
_____
_____
_____
_____
_____
_____
_____
_____
_____
_____
_____
_____
_____
_____
_____
_____
_____
_____
_____
_____
_____
_____
_____
_____
_____
_____
_____
_____
_____
_____

Today's Date: _____

What is your grief level from 0-10, with ten being the strongest? _____

What is your dominate felling, emotion, or mood today?
_____

What are your thoughts today?

_____
_____
_____
_____
_____
_____
_____
_____
_____
_____
_____
_____
_____
_____
_____
_____
_____
_____
_____
_____
_____
_____
_____
_____
_____
_____
_____

Today's Date: _____

What is your grief level from 0-10, with ten being the
strongest? _____

What is your dominate feeling, emotion, or mood today?
_____

What are your thoughts today?

_____
_____
_____
_____
_____
_____
_____
_____
_____
_____
_____
_____
_____
_____
_____
_____
_____
_____
_____
_____
_____
_____
_____
_____
_____
_____

Today's Date: _____

What is your grief level from 0-10, with ten being the strongest? _____

What is your dominate felling, emotion, or mood today?

_____

What are your thoughts today?

_____

_____

_____

_____

_____

_____

_____

_____

_____

_____

_____

_____

_____

_____

_____

_____

_____

_____

_____

_____

_____

_____

_____

_____

_____

_____

_____

_____

Today's Date: _____

What is your grief level from 0-10, with ten being the
strongest? _____

What is your dominate feeling, emotion, or mood today?
_____

What are your thoughts today?

_____
_____
_____
_____
_____
_____
_____
_____
_____
_____
_____
_____
_____
_____
_____
_____
_____
_____
_____
_____
_____
_____
_____
_____
_____
_____
_____
_____
_____
_____
_____

Today's Date: _____

What is your grief level from 0-10, with ten being the
strongest? _____

What is your dominate felling, emotion, or mood today?

_____

What are your thoughts today?

_____

_____

_____

_____

_____

_____

_____

_____

_____

_____

_____

_____

_____

_____

_____

_____

_____

_____

_____

_____

_____

_____

_____

_____

_____

_____

_____

_____

_____

_____

Today's Date: _____

What is your grief level from 0-10, with ten being the
strongest? _____

What is your dominate feeling, emotion, or mood today?
_____

What are your thoughts today?

_____
_____
_____
_____
_____
_____
_____
_____
_____
_____
_____
_____
_____
_____
_____
_____
_____
_____
_____
_____
_____
_____
_____
_____
_____
_____
_____

Today's Date: _____

What is your grief level from 0-10, with ten being the strongest? _____

What is your dominate felling, emotion, or mood today?
_____

What are your thoughts today?

_____
_____
_____
_____
_____
_____
_____
_____
_____
_____
_____
_____
_____
_____
_____
_____
_____
_____
_____
_____
_____
_____
_____
_____
_____
_____
_____
_____
_____
_____
_____

Today's Date: _____

What is your grief level from 0-10, with ten being the strongest? _____

What is your dominate feeling, emotion, or mood today? _____

What are your thoughts today?

_____
_____
_____
_____
_____
_____
_____
_____
_____
_____
_____
_____
_____
_____
_____
_____
_____
_____
_____
_____
_____
_____
_____
_____
_____
_____
_____
_____
_____

Today's Date: _____

What is your grief level from 0-10, with ten being the strongest? _____

What is your dominate feeling, emotion, or mood today?
_____

What are your thoughts today?

_____
_____
_____
_____
_____
_____
_____
_____
_____
_____
_____
_____
_____
_____
_____
_____
_____
_____
_____
_____
_____
_____
_____
_____
_____
_____
_____

Today's Date: _____

What is your grief level from 0-10, with ten being the strongest? _____

What is your dominate feeling, emotion, or mood today?
_____

What are your thoughts today?

_____
_____
_____
_____
_____
_____
_____
_____
_____
_____
_____
_____
_____
_____
_____
_____
_____
_____
_____
_____
_____
_____
_____
_____
_____
_____
_____
_____
_____

Today's Date: _____

What is your grief level from 0-10, with ten being the strongest? _____

What is your dominate feeling, emotion, or mood today? _____

What are your thoughts today?

_____

_____

_____

_____

_____

_____

_____

_____

_____

_____

_____

_____

_____

_____

_____

_____

_____

_____

_____

_____

_____

_____

_____

_____

_____

_____

_____

_____

Today's Date: _____

What is your grief level from 0-10, with ten being the
strongest? _____

What is your dominate feeling, emotion, or mood today?
_____

What are your thoughts today?

_____
_____
_____
_____
_____
_____
_____
_____
_____
_____
_____
_____
_____
_____
_____
_____
_____
_____
_____
_____
_____
_____
_____
_____
_____
_____
_____
_____

Today's Date: _____

What is your grief level from 0-10, with ten being the
strongest? _____

What is your dominate feeling, emotion, or mood today?
_____

What are your thoughts today?

_____
_____
_____
_____
_____
_____
_____
_____
_____
_____
_____
_____
_____
_____
_____
_____
_____
_____
_____
_____
_____
_____
_____
_____
_____
_____
_____
_____

Today's Date: _____

What is your grief level from 0-10, with ten being the strongest? _____

What is your dominate feeling, emotion, or mood today?
_____

What are your thoughts today?

_____
_____
_____
_____
_____
_____
_____
_____
_____
_____
_____
_____
_____
_____
_____
_____
_____
_____
_____
_____
_____
_____
_____
_____
_____
_____
_____
_____
_____

Today's Date: _____

What is your grief level from 0-10, with ten being the strongest? _____

What is your dominate feeling, emotion, or mood today?

_____

What are your thoughts today?

_____

_____

_____

_____

_____

_____

_____

_____

_____

_____

_____

_____

_____

_____

_____

_____

_____

_____

_____

_____

_____

_____

_____

_____

_____

_____

_____

_____

_____

_____

_____

_____

_____

_____

Today's Date: _____

What is your grief level from 0-10, with ten being the strongest? _____

What is your dominate feeling, emotion, or mood today?
_____

What are your thoughts today?

_____
_____
_____
_____
_____
_____
_____
_____
_____
_____
_____
_____
_____
_____
_____
_____
_____
_____
_____
_____
_____
_____
_____
_____
_____
_____
_____
_____

Today's Date: _____

What is your grief level from 0-10, with ten being the strongest? _____

What is your dominate feeling, emotion, or mood today?
_____

What are your thoughts today?

_____

_____

_____

_____

_____

_____

_____

_____

_____

_____

_____

_____

_____

_____

_____

_____

_____

_____

_____

_____

_____

_____

_____

_____

_____

_____

_____

_____

_____

Today's Date: _____

What is your grief level from 0-10, with ten being the strongest? _____

What is your dominate feeling, emotion, or mood today? _____

What are your thoughts today?

_____
_____
_____
_____
_____
_____
_____
_____
_____
_____
_____
_____
_____
_____
_____
_____
_____
_____
_____
_____
_____
_____
_____
_____
_____
_____
_____
_____

Today's Date: _____

What is your grief level from 0-10, with ten being the strongest? _____

What is your dominate feeling, emotion, or mood today?
_____

What are your thoughts today?

_____

_____

_____

_____

_____

_____

_____

_____

_____

_____

_____

_____

_____

_____

_____

_____

_____

_____

_____

_____

_____

_____

_____

_____

_____

_____

_____

_____

_____

_____

Today's Date: _____

What is your grief level from 0-10, with ten being the strongest? _____

What is your dominate feeling, emotion, or mood today? _____

What are your thoughts today?

_____
_____
_____
_____
_____
_____
_____
_____
_____
_____
_____
_____
_____
_____
_____
_____
_____
_____
_____
_____
_____
_____
_____
_____
_____
_____
_____
_____

Today's Date: _____

What is your grief level from 0-10, with ten being the strongest? _____

What is your dominate feeling, emotion, or mood today?
_____

What are your thoughts today?

_____
_____
_____
_____
_____
_____
_____
_____
_____
_____
_____
_____
_____
_____
_____
_____
_____
_____
_____
_____
_____
_____
_____
_____
_____
_____
_____
_____
_____

Today's Date: _____

What is your grief level from 0-10, with ten being the strongest? _____

What is your dominate feeling, emotion, or mood today? _____

What are your thoughts today?

_____
_____
_____
_____
_____
_____
_____
_____
_____
_____
_____
_____
_____
_____
_____
_____
_____
_____
_____
_____
_____
_____
_____
_____
_____
_____
_____

Today's Date: _____

What is your grief level from 0-10, with ten being the strongest? _____

What is your dominate feeling, emotion, or mood today? _____

What are your thoughts today?

_____

_____

_____

_____

_____

_____

_____

_____

_____

_____

_____

_____

_____

_____

_____

_____

_____

_____

_____

_____

_____

_____

_____

_____

_____

_____

_____

Today's Date: _____

What is your grief level from 0-10, with ten being the strongest? _____

What is your dominate feeling, emotion, or mood today? _____

What are your thoughts today?

_____
_____
_____
_____
_____
_____
_____
_____
_____
_____
_____
_____
_____
_____
_____
_____
_____
_____
_____
_____
_____
_____
_____
_____
_____
_____
_____
_____

Today's Date: _____

What is your grief level from 0-10, with ten being the strongest? _____

What is your dominate feeling, emotion, or mood today? _____

What are your thoughts today?

_____

_____

_____

_____

_____

_____

_____

_____

_____

_____

_____

_____

_____

_____

_____

_____

_____

_____

_____

_____

_____

_____

_____

_____

_____

_____

_____

_____

_____

_____

Today's Date: _____

What is your grief level from 0-10, with ten being the strongest? _____

What is your dominate feeling, emotion, or mood today? _____

What are your thoughts today?

_____
_____
_____
_____
_____
_____
_____
_____
_____
_____
_____
_____
_____
_____
_____
_____
_____
_____
_____
_____
_____
_____
_____
_____
_____
_____
_____
_____

Today's Date: _____

What is your grief level from 0-10, with ten being the strongest? _____

What is your dominate feeling, emotion, or mood today?
_____

What are your thoughts today?

_____

_____

_____

_____

_____

_____

_____

_____

_____

_____

_____

_____

_____

_____

_____

_____

_____

_____

_____

_____

_____

_____

_____

_____

_____

_____

_____

_____

_____

Today's Date: _____

What is your grief level from 0-10, with ten being the strongest? _____

What is your dominate feeling, emotion, or mood today? _____

What are your thoughts today?

_____

_____

_____

_____

_____

_____

_____

_____

_____

_____

_____

_____

_____

_____

_____

_____

_____

_____

_____

_____

_____

_____

_____

_____

_____

Monthly Motivation #9

Romans 5:1-4 1. Therefore being justified by faith we have peace with God through our Lord Jesus Christ: 2. By whom we also have access by faith into this grace wherein we stand, and rejoice in hope of the glory of God. 3. And not only so, but we glory in tribulations also: knowing that tribulation worketh patience. 4. And patience, experience: and experience, hope.

~KJV

Today's Date: _____

What is your grief level from 0-10, with ten being the strongest? _____

What is your dominate feeling, emotion, or mood today?
_____

What are your thoughts today?

_____
_____
_____
_____
_____
_____
_____
_____
_____
_____
_____
_____
_____
_____
_____
_____
_____
_____
_____
_____
_____
_____
_____
_____
_____
_____
_____
_____
_____

Today's Date: _____

What is your grief level from 0-10, with ten being the strongest? _____

What is your dominate felling, emotion, or mood today?

_____

What are your thoughts today?

_____

_____

_____

_____

_____

_____

_____

_____

_____

_____

_____

_____

_____

_____

_____

_____

_____

_____

_____

_____

_____

_____

_____

_____

_____

_____

_____

_____

_____

_____

Today's Date: _____

What is your grief level from 0-10, with ten being the strongest? _____

What is your dominate feeling, emotion, or mood today? _____

What are your thoughts today?

_____

_____

_____

_____

_____

_____

_____

_____

_____

_____

_____

_____

_____

_____

_____

_____

_____

_____

_____

_____

_____

_____

_____

_____

_____

_____

_____

Today's Date: _____

What is your grief level from 0-10, with ten being the strongest? _____

What is your dominate felling, emotion, or mood today? _____

What are your thoughts today?

_____
_____
_____
_____
_____
_____
_____
_____
_____
_____
_____
_____
_____
_____
_____
_____
_____
_____
_____
_____
_____
_____
_____
_____
_____
_____
_____
_____
_____

Today's Date: _____

What is your grief level from 0-10, with ten being the strongest? _____

What is your dominate feeling, emotion, or mood today? _____

What are your thoughts today?

_____
_____
_____
_____
_____
_____
_____
_____
_____
_____
_____
_____
_____
_____
_____
_____
_____
_____
_____
_____
_____
_____
_____
_____
_____
_____
_____
_____
_____
_____

Today's Date: _____

What is your grief level from 0-10, with ten being the strongest? _____

What is your dominate felling, emotion, or mood today?
_____

What are your thoughts today?

_____
_____
_____
_____
_____
_____
_____
_____
_____
_____
_____
_____
_____
_____
_____
_____
_____
_____
_____
_____
_____
_____
_____
_____
_____
_____
_____
_____

Today's Date: _____

What is your grief level from 0-10, with ten being the strongest? _____

What is your dominate feeling, emotion, or mood today? _____

What are your thoughts today?

_____
_____
_____
_____
_____
_____
_____
_____
_____
_____
_____
_____
_____
_____
_____
_____
_____
_____
_____
_____
_____
_____
_____
_____
_____
_____
_____
_____
_____
_____

Today's Date: _____

What is your grief level from 0-10, with ten being the strongest? _____

What is your dominate felling, emotion, or mood today? _____

What are your thoughts today?

_____

_____

_____

_____

_____

_____

_____

_____

_____

_____

_____

_____

_____

_____

_____

_____

_____

_____

_____

_____

_____

_____

_____

_____

_____

_____

_____

_____

Today's Date: _____

What is your grief level from 0-10, with ten being the strongest? _____

What is your dominate feeling, emotion, or mood today?
_____

What are your thoughts today?

_____
_____
_____
_____
_____
_____
_____
_____
_____
_____
_____
_____
_____
_____
_____
_____
_____
_____
_____
_____
_____
_____
_____
_____
_____
_____
_____

Today's Date: _____

What is your grief level from 0-10, with ten being the strongest? _____

What is your dominate felling, emotion, or mood today? _____

What are your thoughts today?

_____

_____

_____

_____

_____

_____

_____

_____

_____

_____

_____

_____

_____

_____

_____

_____

_____

_____

_____

_____

_____

_____

_____

_____

_____

_____

_____

_____

Today's Date: _____

What is your grief level from 0-10, with ten being the strongest? _____

What is your dominate feeling, emotion, or mood today? _____

What are your thoughts today?

_____
_____
_____
_____
_____
_____
_____
_____
_____
_____
_____
_____
_____
_____
_____
_____
_____
_____
_____
_____
_____
_____
_____
_____
_____
_____
_____
_____
_____
_____

Today's Date: _____

What is your grief level from 0-10, with ten being the strongest? _____

What is your dominate feeling, emotion, or mood today?
_____

What are your thoughts today?

_____
_____
_____
_____
_____
_____
_____
_____
_____
_____
_____
_____
_____
_____
_____
_____
_____
_____
_____
_____
_____
_____
_____
_____
_____
_____
_____
_____

Today's Date: _____

What is your grief level from 0-10, with ten being the strongest? _____

What is your dominate feeling, emotion, or mood today? _____

What are your thoughts today?

_____
_____
_____
_____
_____
_____
_____
_____
_____
_____
_____
_____
_____
_____
_____
_____
_____
_____
_____
_____
_____
_____
_____
_____
_____
_____
_____
_____
_____
_____

Today's Date: _____

What is your grief level from 0-10, with ten being the strongest? _____

What is your dominate feeling, emotion, or mood today?
_____

What are your thoughts today?

_____

_____

_____

_____

_____

_____

_____

_____

_____

_____

_____

_____

_____

_____

_____

_____

_____

_____

_____

_____

_____

_____

_____

_____

_____

_____

_____

Today's Date: _____

What is your grief level from 0-10, with ten being the
strongest? _____

What is your dominate feeling, emotion, or mood today?
_____

What are your thoughts today?

_____
_____
_____
_____
_____
_____
_____
_____
_____
_____
_____
_____
_____
_____
_____
_____
_____
_____
_____
_____
_____
_____
_____
_____
_____
_____
_____
_____
_____
_____

Today's Date: _____

What is your grief level from 0-10, with ten being the strongest? _____

What is your dominate feeling, emotion, or mood today?
_____

What are your thoughts today?

_____

_____

_____

_____

_____

_____

_____

_____

_____

_____

_____

_____

_____

_____

_____

_____

_____

_____

_____

_____

_____

_____

_____

_____

_____

_____

_____

_____

_____

Today's Date: _____

What is your grief level from 0-10, with ten being the strongest? _____

What is your dominate feeling, emotion, or mood today?
_____

What are your thoughts today?

_____
_____
_____
_____
_____
_____
_____
_____
_____
_____
_____
_____
_____
_____
_____
_____
_____
_____
_____
_____
_____
_____
_____
_____
_____
_____
_____
_____

Today's Date: _____

What is your grief level from 0-10, with ten being the strongest? _____

What is your dominate feeling, emotion, or mood today?

_____

What are your thoughts today?

_____

_____

_____

_____

_____

_____

_____

_____

_____

_____

_____

_____

_____

_____

_____

_____

_____

_____

_____

_____

_____

_____

_____

_____

_____

_____

_____

Today's Date: _____

What is your grief level from 0-10, with ten being the strongest? _____

What is your dominate feeling, emotion, or mood today?
_____

What are your thoughts today?

_____
_____
_____
_____
_____
_____
_____
_____
_____
_____
_____
_____
_____
_____
_____
_____
_____
_____
_____
_____
_____
_____
_____
_____
_____
_____
_____
_____
_____
_____

Today's Date: _____

What is your grief level from 0-10, with ten being the strongest? _____

What is your dominate feeling, emotion, or mood today?

_____

What are your thoughts today?

_____

_____

_____

_____

_____

_____

_____

_____

_____

_____

_____

_____

_____

_____

_____

_____

_____

_____

_____

_____

_____

_____

_____

_____

_____

_____

_____

_____

_____

_____

_____

_____

Today's Date: _____

What is your grief level from 0-10, with ten being the strongest? _____

What is your dominate feeling, emotion, or mood today? _____

What are your thoughts today?

_____
_____
_____
_____
_____
_____
_____
_____
_____
_____
_____
_____
_____
_____
_____
_____
_____
_____
_____
_____
_____
_____
_____
_____
_____
_____
_____
_____

Today's Date: _____

What is your grief level from 0-10, with ten being the strongest? _____

What is your dominate feeling, emotion, or mood today?
_____

What are your thoughts today?

_____
_____
_____
_____
_____
_____
_____
_____
_____
_____
_____
_____
_____
_____
_____
_____
_____
_____
_____
_____
_____
_____
_____
_____
_____
_____
_____
_____

Today's Date: _____

What is your grief level from 0-10, with ten being the
strongest? _____

What is your dominate feeling, emotion, or mood today?
_____

What are your thoughts today?

_____
_____
_____
_____
_____
_____
_____
_____
_____
_____
_____
_____
_____
_____
_____
_____
_____
_____
_____
_____
_____
_____
_____
_____
_____
_____
_____
_____
_____

Today's Date: _____

What is your grief level from 0-10, with ten being the strongest? _____

What is your dominate feeling, emotion, or mood today? _____

What are your thoughts today?

_____
_____
_____
_____
_____
_____
_____
_____
_____
_____
_____
_____
_____
_____
_____
_____
_____
_____
_____
_____
_____
_____
_____
_____
_____
_____
_____
_____
_____

Today's Date: _____

What is your grief level from 0-10, with ten being the strongest? _____

What is your dominate feeling, emotion, or mood today?
_____

What are your thoughts today?

_____
_____
_____
_____
_____
_____
_____
_____
_____
_____
_____
_____
_____
_____
_____
_____
_____
_____
_____
_____
_____
_____
_____
_____
_____
_____
_____
_____
_____

Today's Date: _____

What is your grief level from 0-10, with ten being the strongest? _____

What is your dominate feeling, emotion, or mood today? _____

What are your thoughts today?

_____
_____
_____
_____
_____
_____
_____
_____
_____
_____
_____
_____
_____
_____
_____
_____
_____
_____
_____
_____
_____
_____
_____
_____
_____
_____
_____
_____

Today's Date: _____

What is your grief level from 0-10, with ten being the strongest? _____

What is your dominate feeling, emotion, or mood today? _____

What are your thoughts today?

_____
_____
_____
_____
_____
_____
_____
_____
_____
_____
_____
_____
_____
_____
_____
_____
_____
_____
_____
_____
_____
_____
_____
_____
_____
_____
_____
_____

Today's Date: _____

What is your grief level from 0-10, with ten being the strongest? _____

What is your dominate feeling, emotion, or mood today?
_____

What are your thoughts today?

_____
_____
_____
_____
_____
_____
_____
_____
_____
_____
_____
_____
_____
_____
_____
_____
_____
_____
_____
_____
_____
_____
_____
_____
_____
_____
_____
_____
_____
_____
_____
_____

Today's Date: _____

What is your grief level from 0-10, with ten being the strongest? _____

What is your dominate feeling, emotion, or mood today? _____

What are your thoughts today?

_____
_____
_____
_____
_____
_____
_____
_____
_____
_____
_____
_____
_____
_____
_____
_____
_____
_____
_____
_____
_____
_____
_____
_____
_____
_____
_____
_____
_____

Today's Date: _____

What is your grief level from 0-10, with ten being the strongest? _____

What is your dominate feeling, emotion, or mood today?

_____

What are your thoughts today?

_____

_____

_____

_____

_____

_____

_____

_____

_____

_____

_____

_____

_____

_____

_____

_____

_____

_____

_____

_____

_____

_____

_____

_____

_____

_____

_____

_____

_____

_____

Today's Date: _____

What is your grief level from 0-10, with ten being the strongest? _____

What is your dominate feeling, emotion, or mood today? _____

What are your thoughts today?

_____

_____

_____

_____

_____

_____

_____

_____

_____

_____

_____

_____

_____

_____

_____

_____

_____

_____

_____

_____

_____

_____

_____

_____

_____

_____

_____

_____

When you are saved and your loved one is saved, the separation is a short and temporary one. Praise Jesus! Hallelujah!

~Lisa Mikell

Today's Date: _____

What is your grief level from 0-10, with ten being the
strongest? _____

What is your dominate feeling, emotion, or mood today?
_____

What are your thoughts today?

_____
_____
_____
_____
_____
_____
_____
_____
_____
_____
_____
_____
_____
_____
_____
_____
_____
_____
_____
_____
_____
_____
_____
_____
_____
_____
_____
_____

Today's Date: _____

What is your grief level from 0-10, with ten being the strongest? _____

What is your dominate felling, emotion, or mood today? _____

What are your thoughts today?

_____

_____

_____

_____

_____

_____

_____

_____

_____

_____

_____

_____

_____

_____

_____

_____

_____

_____

_____

_____

_____

_____

_____

_____

_____

_____

_____

_____

_____

Today's Date: _____

What is your grief level from 0-10, with ten being the strongest? _____

What is your dominate feeling, emotion, or mood today? _____

What are your thoughts today?

_____
_____
_____
_____
_____
_____
_____
_____
_____
_____
_____
_____
_____
_____
_____
_____
_____
_____
_____
_____
_____
_____
_____
_____
_____
_____
_____
_____
_____

Today's Date: _____

What is your grief level from 0-10, with ten being the strongest? _____

What is your dominate felling, emotion, or mood today? _____

What are your thoughts today?

_____
_____
_____
_____
_____
_____
_____
_____
_____
_____
_____
_____
_____
_____
_____
_____
_____
_____
_____
_____
_____
_____
_____
_____
_____
_____
_____
_____
_____
_____

Today's Date: _____

What is your grief level from 0-10, with ten being the
strongest? _____

What is your dominate feeling, emotion, or mood today?
_____

What are your thoughts today?

_____
_____
_____
_____
_____
_____
_____
_____
_____
_____
_____
_____
_____
_____
_____
_____
_____
_____
_____
_____
_____
_____
_____
_____
_____
_____
_____
_____
_____

Today's Date: _____

What is your grief level from 0-10, with ten being the strongest? _____

What is your dominate felling, emotion, or mood today?
_____

What are your thoughts today?

_____
_____
_____
_____
_____
_____
_____
_____
_____
_____
_____
_____
_____
_____
_____
_____
_____
_____
_____
_____
_____
_____
_____
_____
_____
_____
_____
_____

Today's Date: _____

What is your grief level from 0-10, with ten being the strongest? _____

What is your dominate feeling, emotion, or mood today? _____

What are your thoughts today?

_____

_____

_____

_____

_____

_____

_____

_____

_____

_____

_____

_____

_____

_____

_____

_____

_____

_____

_____

_____

_____

_____

_____

_____

_____

_____

_____

_____

Today's Date: _____

What is your grief level from 0-10, with ten being the strongest? _____

What is your dominate felling, emotion, or mood today?

_____

What are your thoughts today?

_____

_____

_____

_____

_____

_____

_____

_____

_____

_____

_____

_____

_____

_____

_____

_____

_____

_____

_____

_____

_____

_____

_____

_____

_____

_____

_____

_____

_____

_____

_____

Today's Date: _____

What is your grief level from 0-10, with ten being the strongest? _____

What is your dominate feeling, emotion, or mood today? _____

What are your thoughts today?

_____
_____
_____
_____
_____
_____
_____
_____
_____
_____
_____
_____
_____
_____
_____
_____
_____
_____
_____
_____
_____
_____
_____
_____
_____
_____
_____
_____
_____

Today's Date: _____

What is your grief level from 0-10, with ten being the
strongest? _____

What is your dominate felling, emotion, or mood today?
_____

What are your thoughts today?

_____

_____

_____

_____

_____

_____

_____

_____

_____

_____

_____

_____

_____

_____

_____

_____

_____

_____

_____

_____

_____

_____

_____

_____

_____

_____

_____

_____

_____

Today's Date: _____

What is your grief level from 0-10, with ten being the strongest? _____

What is your dominate feeling, emotion, or mood today? _____

What are your thoughts today?

_____
_____
_____
_____
_____
_____
_____
_____
_____
_____
_____
_____
_____
_____
_____
_____
_____
_____
_____
_____
_____
_____
_____
_____
_____
_____
_____

Today's Date: _____

What is your grief level from 0-10, with ten being the strongest? _____

What is your dominate feeling, emotion, or mood today?

_____

What are your thoughts today?

_____

_____

_____

_____

_____

_____

_____

_____

_____

_____

_____

_____

_____

_____

_____

_____

_____

_____

_____

_____

_____

_____

_____

_____

_____

_____

_____

_____

_____

Today's Date: _____

What is your grief level from 0-10, with ten being the strongest? _____

What is your dominate feeling, emotion, or mood today? _____

What are your thoughts today?

_____
_____
_____
_____
_____
_____
_____
_____
_____
_____
_____
_____
_____
_____
_____
_____
_____
_____
_____
_____
_____
_____
_____
_____
_____
_____
_____
_____
_____

Today's Date: _____

What is your grief level from 0-10, with ten being the strongest? _____

What is your dominate feeling, emotion, or mood today?
_____

What are your thoughts today?

_____
_____
_____
_____
_____
_____
_____
_____
_____
_____
_____
_____
_____
_____
_____
_____
_____
_____
_____
_____
_____
_____
_____
_____
_____
_____
_____
_____

Today's Date: _____

What is your grief level from 0-10, with ten being the strongest? _____

What is your dominate feeling, emotion, or mood today? _____

What are your thoughts today?

_____

Today's Date: _____

What is your grief level from 0-10, with ten being the strongest? _____

What is your dominate feeling, emotion, or mood today?
_____

What are your thoughts today?

_____
_____
_____
_____
_____
_____
_____
_____
_____
_____
_____
_____
_____
_____
_____
_____
_____
_____
_____
_____
_____
_____
_____
_____
_____
_____
_____
_____
_____

Today's Date: _____

What is your grief level from 0-10, with ten being the strongest? _____

What is your dominate feeling, emotion, or mood today? _____

What are your thoughts today?

_____
_____
_____
_____
_____
_____
_____
_____
_____
_____
_____
_____
_____
_____
_____
_____
_____
_____
_____
_____
_____
_____
_____
_____
_____

Today's Date: _____

What is your grief level from 0-10, with ten being the strongest? _____

What is your dominate feeling, emotion, or mood today?

_____

What are your thoughts today?

_____

_____

_____

_____

_____

_____

_____

_____

_____

_____

_____

_____

_____

_____

_____

_____

_____

_____

_____

_____

_____

_____

_____

_____

_____

_____

_____

_____

Today's Date: _____

What is your grief level from 0-10, with ten being the strongest? _____

What is your dominate feeling, emotion, or mood today? _____

What are your thoughts today?

_____
_____
_____
_____
_____
_____
_____
_____
_____
_____
_____
_____
_____
_____
_____
_____
_____
_____
_____
_____
_____
_____
_____
_____
_____
_____
_____
_____

Today's Date: _____

What is your grief level from 0-10, with ten being the
strongest? _____

What is your dominate feeling, emotion, or mood today?
_____

What are your thoughts today?

_____
_____
_____
_____
_____
_____
_____
_____
_____
_____
_____
_____
_____
_____
_____
_____
_____
_____
_____
_____
_____
_____
_____
_____
_____
_____
_____
_____
_____

Today's Date: _____

What is your grief level from 0-10, with ten being the strongest? _____

What is your dominate feeling, emotion, or mood today?
_____

What are your thoughts today?

_____
_____
_____
_____
_____
_____
_____
_____
_____
_____
_____
_____
_____
_____
_____
_____
_____
_____
_____
_____
_____
_____
_____
_____
_____
_____

Today's Date: _____

What is your grief level from 0-10, with ten being the strongest? _____

What is your dominate feeling, emotion, or mood today?

_____

What are your thoughts today?

_____
_____
_____
_____
_____
_____
_____
_____
_____
_____
_____
_____
_____
_____
_____
_____
_____
_____
_____
_____
_____
_____
_____
_____
_____
_____
_____
_____
_____
_____
_____

Today's Date: _____

What is your grief level from 0-10, with ten being the strongest? _____

What is your dominate feeling, emotion, or mood today? _____

What are your thoughts today?

_____

_____

_____

_____

_____

_____

_____

_____

_____

_____

_____

_____

_____

_____

_____

_____

_____

_____

_____

_____

_____

_____

_____

_____

_____

_____

_____

_____

_____

Today's Date: _____

What is your grief level from 0-10, with ten being the
strongest? _____

What is your dominate feeling, emotion, or mood today?
_____

What are your thoughts today?

_____
_____
_____
_____
_____
_____
_____
_____
_____
_____
_____
_____
_____
_____
_____
_____
_____
_____
_____
_____
_____
_____
_____
_____
_____
_____
_____

Today's Date: _____

What is your grief level from 0-10, with ten being the strongest? _____

What is your dominate feeling, emotion, or mood today? _____

What are your thoughts today?

_____
_____
_____
_____
_____
_____
_____
_____
_____
_____
_____
_____
_____
_____
_____
_____
_____
_____
_____
_____
_____
_____
_____
_____
_____
_____
_____
_____
_____

Today's Date: _____

What is your grief level from 0-10, with ten being the strongest? _____

What is your dominate feeling, emotion, or mood today?
_____

What are your thoughts today?

_____
_____
_____
_____
_____
_____
_____
_____
_____
_____
_____
_____
_____
_____
_____
_____
_____
_____
_____
_____
_____
_____
_____
_____
_____
_____
_____
_____

Today's Date: _____

What is your grief level from 0-10, with ten being the strongest? _____

What is your dominate feeling, emotion, or mood today?
_____

What are your thoughts today?

_____
_____
_____
_____
_____
_____
_____
_____
_____
_____
_____
_____
_____
_____
_____
_____
_____
_____
_____
_____
_____
_____
_____
_____
_____
_____
_____
_____
_____

Today's Date: _____

What is your grief level from 0-10, with ten being the strongest? _____

What is your dominate feeling, emotion, or mood today?
_____

What are your thoughts today?

_____

_____

_____

_____

_____

_____

_____

_____

_____

_____

_____

_____

_____

_____

_____

_____

_____

_____

_____

_____

_____

_____

_____

_____

_____

_____

_____

_____

_____

_____

_____

Today's Date: _____

What is your grief level from 0-10, with ten being the strongest? _____

What is your dominate feeling, emotion, or mood today?
_____

What are your thoughts today?

_____
_____
_____
_____
_____
_____
_____
_____
_____
_____
_____
_____
_____
_____
_____
_____
_____
_____
_____
_____
_____
_____
_____
_____
_____
_____
_____
_____
_____

Today's Date: _____

What is your grief level from 0-10, with ten being the
strongest? _____

What is your dominate feeling, emotion, or mood today?
_____

What are your thoughts today?

_____
_____
_____
_____
_____
_____
_____
_____
_____
_____
_____
_____
_____
_____
_____
_____
_____
_____
_____
_____
_____
_____
_____
_____
_____
_____
_____
_____
_____

Today's Date: _____

What is your grief level from 0-10, with ten being the strongest? _____

What is your dominate feeling, emotion, or mood today? _____

What are your thoughts today?

_____
_____
_____
_____
_____
_____
_____
_____
_____
_____
_____
_____
_____
_____
_____
_____
_____
_____
_____
_____
_____
_____
_____
_____
_____
_____
_____
_____

Romans 15:13 Now the God of hope fill you with all joy and peace in believing, that ye may abound in hope, through the power of the Holy Spirit.

~KJV

Today's Date: _____

What is your grief level from 0-10, with ten being the
strongest? _____

What is your dominate feeling, emotion, or mood today?
_____

What are your thoughts today?

_____
_____
_____
_____
_____
_____
_____
_____
_____
_____
_____
_____
_____
_____
_____
_____
_____
_____
_____
_____
_____
_____
_____
_____
_____
_____
_____
_____
_____
_____

Today's Date: _____

What is your grief level from 0-10, with ten being the strongest? _____

What is your dominate felling, emotion, or mood today?
_____

What are your thoughts today?

_____
_____
_____
_____
_____
_____
_____
_____
_____
_____
_____
_____
_____
_____
_____
_____
_____
_____
_____
_____
_____
_____
_____
_____
_____
_____
_____
_____
_____

Today's Date: _____

What is your grief level from 0-10, with ten being the
strongest? _____

What is your dominate feeling, emotion, or mood today?
_____

What are your thoughts today?

_____

_____

_____

_____

_____

_____

_____

_____

_____

_____

_____

_____

_____

_____

_____

_____

_____

_____

_____

_____

_____

_____

_____

_____

_____

_____

_____

Today's Date: _____

What is your grief level from 0-10, with ten being the strongest? _____

What is your dominate felling, emotion, or mood today?
_____

What are your thoughts today?

_____
_____
_____
_____
_____
_____
_____
_____
_____
_____
_____
_____
_____
_____
_____
_____
_____
_____
_____
_____
_____
_____
_____
_____
_____
_____
_____
_____
_____

Today's Date: _____

What is your grief level from 0-10, with ten being the strongest? _____

What is your dominate feeling, emotion, or mood today?
_____

What are your thoughts today?

_____
_____
_____
_____
_____
_____
_____
_____
_____
_____
_____
_____
_____
_____
_____
_____
_____
_____
_____
_____
_____
_____
_____
_____
_____
_____
_____
_____

Today's Date: _____

What is your grief level from 0-10, with ten being the strongest? _____

What is your dominate felling, emotion, or mood today?
_____

What are your thoughts today?

_____
_____
_____
_____
_____
_____
_____
_____
_____
_____
_____
_____
_____
_____
_____
_____
_____
_____
_____
_____
_____
_____
_____
_____
_____
_____
_____
_____
_____

Today's Date: _____

What is your grief level from 0-10, with ten being the strongest? _____

What is your dominate feeling, emotion, or mood today? _____

What are your thoughts today?

_____
_____
_____
_____
_____
_____
_____
_____
_____
_____
_____
_____
_____
_____
_____
_____
_____
_____
_____
_____
_____
_____
_____
_____
_____
_____
_____

Today's Date: _____

What is your grief level from 0-10, with ten being the strongest? _____

What is your dominate felling, emotion, or mood today?

_____

What are your thoughts today?

_____

_____

_____

_____

_____

_____

_____

_____

_____

_____

_____

_____

_____

_____

_____

_____

_____

_____

_____

_____

_____

_____

_____

_____

_____

_____

_____

_____

Today's Date: _____

What is your grief level from 0-10, with ten being the strongest? _____

What is your dominate feeling, emotion, or mood today? _____

What are your thoughts today?

_____
_____
_____
_____
_____
_____
_____
_____
_____
_____
_____
_____
_____
_____
_____
_____
_____
_____
_____
_____
_____
_____
_____
_____
_____
_____
_____
_____

Today's Date: _____

What is your grief level from 0-10, with ten being the strongest? _____

What is your dominate felling, emotion, or mood today?
_____

What are your thoughts today?

_____
_____
_____
_____
_____
_____
_____
_____
_____
_____
_____
_____
_____
_____
_____
_____
_____
_____
_____
_____
_____
_____
_____
_____
_____
_____
_____
_____
_____
_____
_____

Today's Date: _____

What is your grief level from 0-10, with ten being the strongest? _____

What is your dominate feeling, emotion, or mood today?
_____

What are your thoughts today?

_____

_____

_____

_____

_____

_____

_____

_____

_____

_____

_____

_____

_____

_____

_____

_____

_____

_____

_____

_____

_____

_____

_____

_____

_____

_____

_____

_____

_____

Today's Date: _____

What is your grief level from 0-10, with ten being the
strongest? _____

What is your dominate feeling, emotion, or mood today?
_____

What are your thoughts today?

_____
_____
_____
_____
_____
_____
_____
_____
_____
_____
_____
_____
_____
_____
_____
_____
_____
_____
_____
_____
_____
_____
_____
_____
_____
_____
_____
_____

Today's Date: _____

What is your grief level from 0-10, with ten being the strongest? _____

What is your dominate feeling, emotion, or mood today?
_____

What are your thoughts today?

_____
_____
_____
_____
_____
_____
_____
_____
_____
_____
_____
_____
_____
_____
_____
_____
_____
_____
_____
_____
_____
_____
_____
_____
_____
_____
_____
_____

Today's Date: _____

What is your grief level from 0-10, with ten being the strongest? _____

What is your dominate feeling, emotion, or mood today?
_____

What are your thoughts today?

_____
_____
_____
_____
_____
_____
_____
_____
_____
_____
_____
_____
_____
_____
_____
_____
_____
_____
_____
_____
_____
_____
_____
_____
_____
_____
_____
_____
_____
_____

Today's Date: _____

What is your grief level from 0-10, with ten being the strongest? _____

What is your dominate feeling, emotion, or mood today? _____

What are your thoughts today?

_____
_____
_____
_____
_____
_____
_____
_____
_____
_____
_____
_____
_____
_____
_____
_____
_____
_____
_____
_____
_____
_____
_____
_____
_____
_____
_____
_____
_____

Today's Date: _____

What is your grief level from 0-10, with ten being the strongest? _____

What is your dominate feeling, emotion, or mood today?
_____

What are your thoughts today?

_____
_____
_____
_____
_____
_____
_____
_____
_____
_____
_____
_____
_____
_____
_____
_____
_____
_____
_____
_____
_____
_____
_____
_____
_____
_____
_____
_____
_____
_____

Today's Date: _____

What is your grief level from 0-10, with ten being the strongest? _____

What is your dominate feeling, emotion, or mood today?
_____

What are your thoughts today?

_____
_____
_____
_____
_____
_____
_____
_____
_____
_____
_____
_____
_____
_____
_____
_____
_____
_____
_____
_____
_____
_____
_____
_____
_____
_____
_____
_____
_____

Today's Date: _____

What is your grief level from 0-10, with ten being the strongest? _____

What is your dominate feeling, emotion, or mood today? _____

What are your thoughts today?

_____
_____
_____
_____
_____
_____
_____
_____
_____
_____
_____
_____
_____
_____
_____
_____
_____
_____
_____
_____
_____
_____
_____
_____
_____
_____
_____
_____
_____

Today's Date: _____

What is your grief level from 0-10, with ten being the strongest? _____

What is your dominate feeling, emotion, or mood today? _____

What are your thoughts today?

_____
_____
_____
_____
_____
_____
_____
_____
_____
_____
_____
_____
_____
_____
_____
_____
_____
_____
_____
_____
_____
_____
_____
_____
_____
_____
_____
_____
_____

Today's Date: _____

What is your grief level from 0-10, with ten being the strongest? _____

What is your dominate feeling, emotion, or mood today?
_____

What are your thoughts today?

_____

_____

_____

_____

_____

_____

_____

_____

_____

_____

_____

_____

_____

_____

_____

_____

_____

_____

_____

_____

_____

_____

_____

_____

_____

_____

_____

_____

Today's Date: _____

What is your grief level from 0-10, with ten being the strongest? _____

What is your dominate feeling, emotion, or mood today?
_____

What are your thoughts today?

_____
_____
_____
_____
_____
_____
_____
_____
_____
_____
_____
_____
_____
_____
_____
_____
_____
_____
_____
_____
_____
_____
_____
_____
_____
_____

Today's Date: _____

What is your grief level from 0-10, with ten being the strongest? _____

What is your dominate feeling, emotion, or mood today?
_____

What are your thoughts today?

_____
_____
_____
_____
_____
_____
_____
_____
_____
_____
_____
_____
_____
_____
_____
_____
_____
_____
_____
_____
_____
_____
_____
_____
_____
_____
_____
_____
_____

Today's Date: _____

What is your grief level from 0-10, with ten being the strongest? _____

What is your dominate feeling, emotion, or mood today? _____

What are your thoughts today?

_____
_____
_____
_____
_____
_____
_____
_____
_____
_____
_____
_____
_____
_____
_____
_____
_____
_____
_____
_____
_____
_____
_____
_____
_____
_____
_____

Today's Date: _____

What is your grief level from 0-10, with ten being the strongest? _____

What is your dominate feeling, emotion, or mood today?
_____

What are your thoughts today?

_____

_____

_____

_____

_____

_____

_____

_____

_____

_____

_____

_____

_____

_____

_____

_____

_____

_____

_____

_____

_____

_____

_____

_____

_____

_____

_____

Today's Date: _____

What is your grief level from 0-10, with ten being the strongest? _____

What is your dominate feeling, emotion, or mood today? _____

What are your thoughts today?

_____
_____
_____
_____
_____
_____
_____
_____
_____
_____
_____
_____
_____
_____
_____
_____
_____
_____
_____
_____
_____
_____
_____
_____
_____
_____
_____
_____

Today's Date: _____

What is your grief level from 0-10, with ten being the strongest? _____

What is your dominate feeling, emotion, or mood today?
_____

What are your thoughts today?

_____
_____
_____
_____
_____
_____
_____
_____
_____
_____
_____
_____
_____
_____
_____
_____
_____
_____
_____
_____
_____
_____
_____
_____
_____
_____
_____
_____
_____
_____

Today's Date: _____

What is your grief level from 0-10, with ten being the strongest? _____

What is your dominate feeling, emotion, or mood today? _____

What are your thoughts today?

_____

_____

_____

_____

_____

_____

_____

_____

_____

_____

_____

_____

_____

_____

_____

_____

_____

_____

_____

_____

_____

_____

_____

_____

_____

_____

_____

_____

_____

Today's Date: _____

What is your grief level from 0-10, with ten being the strongest? _____

What is your dominate feeling, emotion, or mood today?
_____

What are your thoughts today?

_____
_____
_____
_____
_____
_____
_____
_____
_____
_____
_____
_____
_____
_____
_____
_____
_____
_____
_____
_____
_____
_____
_____
_____
_____
_____
_____
_____
_____
_____

Today's Date: _____

What is your grief level from 0-10, with ten being the strongest? _____

What is your dominate feeling, emotion, or mood today? _____

What are your thoughts today?

_____
_____
_____
_____
_____
_____
_____
_____
_____
_____
_____
_____
_____
_____
_____
_____
_____
_____
_____
_____
_____
_____
_____
_____
_____
_____
_____

Today's Date: _____

What is your grief level from 0-10, with ten being the strongest? _____

What is your dominate feeling, emotion, or mood today? _____

What are your thoughts today?

_____

_____

_____

_____

_____

_____

_____

_____

_____

_____

_____

_____

_____

_____

_____

_____

_____

_____

_____

_____

_____

_____

_____

_____

_____

_____

_____

Today's Date: _____

What is your grief level from 0-10, with ten being the strongest? _____

What is your dominate feeling, emotion, or mood today? _____

What are your thoughts today?

_____
_____
_____
_____
_____
_____
_____
_____
_____
_____
_____
_____
_____
_____
_____
_____
_____
_____
_____
_____
_____
_____
_____
_____
_____
_____
_____
_____

You woke up this morning because you received an invitation from God to enjoy this beautiful day. Enjoy it!

~Lisa Mikell

Today's Date: _____

What is your grief level from 0-10, with ten being the strongest? _____

What is your dominate feeling, emotion, or mood today?
_____

What are your thoughts today?

_____
_____
_____
_____
_____
_____
_____
_____
_____
_____
_____
_____
_____
_____
_____
_____
_____
_____
_____
_____
_____
_____
_____
_____
_____
_____
_____
_____
_____

Today's Date: _____

What is your grief level from 0-10, with ten being the strongest? _____

What is your dominate felling, emotion, or mood today? _____

What are your thoughts today?

_____
_____
_____
_____
_____
_____
_____
_____
_____
_____
_____
_____
_____
_____
_____
_____
_____
_____
_____
_____
_____
_____
_____
_____
_____
_____
_____
_____
_____

Today's Date: _____

What is your grief level from 0-10, with ten being the strongest? _____

What is your dominate feeling, emotion, or mood today? _____

What are your thoughts today?

_____
_____
_____
_____
_____
_____
_____
_____
_____
_____
_____
_____
_____
_____
_____
_____
_____
_____
_____
_____
_____
_____
_____
_____
_____
_____
_____
_____
_____

Today's Date: _____

What is your grief level from 0-10, with ten being the strongest? _____

What is your dominate felling, emotion, or mood today?
_____

What are your thoughts today?

_____
_____
_____
_____
_____
_____
_____
_____
_____
_____
_____
_____
_____
_____
_____
_____
_____
_____
_____
_____
_____
_____
_____
_____
_____
_____
_____
_____
_____

Today's Date: _____

What is your grief level from 0-10, with ten being the strongest? _____

What is your dominate feeling, emotion, or mood today? _____

What are your thoughts today?

_____
_____
_____
_____
_____
_____
_____
_____
_____
_____
_____
_____
_____
_____
_____
_____
_____
_____
_____
_____
_____
_____
_____
_____
_____
_____
_____
_____
_____
_____

Today's Date: _____

What is your grief level from 0-10, with ten being the strongest? _____

What is your dominate felling, emotion, or mood today? _____

What are your thoughts today?

_____

_____

_____

_____

_____

_____

_____

_____

_____

_____

_____

_____

_____

_____

_____

_____

_____

_____

_____

_____

_____

_____

_____

_____

_____

_____

_____

_____

Today's Date: _____

What is your grief level from 0-10, with ten being the
strongest? _____

What is your dominate feeling, emotion, or mood today?
_____

What are your thoughts today?

_____
_____
_____
_____
_____
_____
_____
_____
_____
_____
_____
_____
_____
_____
_____
_____
_____
_____
_____
_____
_____
_____
_____
_____
_____
_____
_____
_____
_____

Today's Date: _____

What is your grief level from 0-10, with ten being the strongest? _____

What is your dominate felling, emotion, or mood today?
_____

What are your thoughts today?

_____
_____
_____
_____
_____
_____
_____
_____
_____
_____
_____
_____
_____
_____
_____
_____
_____
_____
_____
_____
_____
_____
_____
_____
_____
_____
_____
_____

Today's Date: _____

What is your grief level from 0-10, with ten being the
strongest? _____

What is your dominate feeling, emotion, or mood today?
_____

What are your thoughts today?

_____
_____
_____
_____
_____
_____
_____
_____
_____
_____
_____
_____
_____
_____
_____
_____
_____
_____
_____
_____
_____
_____
_____
_____
_____
_____
_____

Today's Date: _____

What is your grief level from 0-10, with ten being the strongest? _____

What is your dominate felling, emotion, or mood today? _____

What are your thoughts today?

_____
_____
_____
_____
_____
_____
_____
_____
_____
_____
_____
_____
_____
_____
_____
_____
_____
_____
_____
_____
_____
_____
_____
_____
_____
_____
_____
_____
_____

Today's Date: _____

What is your grief level from 0-10, with ten being the strongest? _____

What is your dominate feeling, emotion, or mood today?
_____

What are your thoughts today?

_____
_____
_____
_____
_____
_____
_____
_____
_____
_____
_____
_____
_____
_____
_____
_____
_____
_____
_____
_____
_____
_____
_____
_____
_____
_____
_____
_____
_____

Today's Date: _____

What is your grief level from 0-10, with ten being the strongest? _____

What is your dominate feeling, emotion, or mood today?
_____

What are your thoughts today?

_____
_____
_____
_____
_____
_____
_____
_____
_____
_____
_____
_____
_____
_____
_____
_____
_____
_____
_____
_____
_____
_____
_____
_____
_____
_____
_____
_____
_____
_____

Today's Date: _____

What is your grief level from 0-10, with ten being the strongest? _____

What is your dominate feeling, emotion, or mood today?
_____

What are your thoughts today?

_____
_____
_____
_____
_____
_____
_____
_____
_____
_____
_____
_____
_____
_____
_____
_____
_____
_____
_____
_____
_____
_____
_____
_____
_____
_____
_____
_____
_____

Today's Date: _____

What is your grief level from 0-10, with ten being the strongest? _____

What is your dominate feeling, emotion, or mood today?
_____

What are your thoughts today?

_____
_____
_____
_____
_____
_____
_____
_____
_____
_____
_____
_____
_____
_____
_____
_____
_____
_____
_____
_____
_____
_____
_____
_____
_____
_____
_____
_____
_____

Today's Date: _____

What is your grief level from 0-10, with ten being the strongest? _____

What is your dominate feeling, emotion, or mood today? _____

What are your thoughts today?

_____
_____
_____
_____
_____
_____
_____
_____
_____
_____
_____
_____
_____
_____
_____
_____
_____
_____
_____
_____
_____
_____
_____
_____
_____
_____
_____
_____

Today's Date: _____

What is your grief level from 0-10, with ten being the strongest? _____

What is your dominate feeling, emotion, or mood today?
_____

What are your thoughts today?

_____
_____
_____
_____
_____
_____
_____
_____
_____
_____
_____
_____
_____
_____
_____
_____
_____
_____
_____
_____
_____
_____
_____
_____
_____
_____
_____

Today's Date: _____

What is your grief level from 0-10, with ten being the strongest? _____

What is your dominate feeling, emotion, or mood today?
_____

What are your thoughts today?

_____
_____
_____
_____
_____
_____
_____
_____
_____
_____
_____
_____
_____
_____
_____
_____
_____
_____
_____
_____
_____
_____
_____
_____
_____
_____
_____
_____
_____
_____

Today's Date: _____

What is your grief level from 0-10, with ten being the
strongest? _____

What is your dominate feeling, emotion, or mood today?
_____

What are your thoughts today?

_____
_____
_____
_____
_____
_____
_____
_____
_____
_____
_____
_____
_____
_____
_____
_____
_____
_____
_____
_____
_____
_____
_____
_____
_____
_____
_____
_____
_____
_____

Today's Date: _____

What is your grief level from 0-10, with ten being the strongest? _____

What is your dominate feeling, emotion, or mood today?
_____

What are your thoughts today?

_____
_____
_____
_____
_____
_____
_____
_____
_____
_____
_____
_____
_____
_____
_____
_____
_____
_____
_____
_____
_____
_____
_____
_____
_____
_____
_____
_____
_____

Today's Date: _____

What is your grief level from 0-10, with ten being the strongest? _____

What is your dominate feeling, emotion, or mood today?
_____

What are your thoughts today?

_____
_____
_____
_____
_____
_____
_____
_____
_____
_____
_____
_____
_____
_____
_____
_____
_____
_____
_____
_____
_____
_____
_____
_____
_____
_____
_____
_____

Today's Date: _____

What is your grief level from 0-10, with ten being the strongest? _____

What is your dominate feeling, emotion, or mood today?
_____

What are your thoughts today?

_____
_____
_____
_____
_____
_____
_____
_____
_____
_____
_____
_____
_____
_____
_____
_____
_____
_____
_____
_____
_____
_____
_____
_____
_____
_____
_____
_____

Today's Date: _____

What is your grief level from 0-10, with ten being the strongest? _____

What is your dominate feeling, emotion, or mood today?
_____

What are your thoughts today?

_____
_____
_____
_____
_____
_____
_____
_____
_____
_____
_____
_____
_____
_____
_____
_____
_____
_____
_____
_____
_____
_____
_____
_____
_____
_____
_____
_____
_____

Today's Date: _____

What is your grief level from 0-10, with ten being the
strongest? _____

What is your dominate feeling, emotion, or mood today?
_____

What are your thoughts today?

_____
_____
_____
_____
_____
_____
_____
_____
_____
_____
_____
_____
_____
_____
_____
_____
_____
_____
_____
_____
_____
_____
_____
_____
_____
_____
_____
_____
_____
_____
_____
_____

Today's Date: _____

What is your grief level from 0-10, with ten being the strongest? _____

What is your dominate feeling, emotion, or mood today?
_____

What are your thoughts today?

_____

_____

_____

_____

_____

_____

_____

_____

_____

_____

_____

_____

_____

_____

_____

_____

_____

_____

_____

_____

_____

_____

_____

_____

_____

_____

_____

_____

Today's Date: _____

What is your grief level from 0-10, with ten being the strongest? _____

What is your dominate feeling, emotion, or mood today? _____

What are your thoughts today?

_____
_____
_____
_____
_____
_____
_____
_____
_____
_____
_____
_____
_____
_____
_____
_____
_____
_____
_____
_____
_____
_____
_____
_____
_____
_____
_____
_____

Today's Date: _____

What is your grief level from 0-10, with ten being the strongest? _____

What is your dominate feeling, emotion, or mood today?
_____

What are your thoughts today?

_____

_____

_____

_____

_____

_____

_____

_____

_____

_____

_____

_____

_____

_____

_____

_____

_____

_____

_____

_____

_____

_____

_____

_____

_____

_____

_____

Today's Date: _____

What is your grief level from 0-10, with ten being the strongest? _____

What is your dominate feeling, emotion, or mood today? _____

What are your thoughts today?

_____
_____
_____
_____
_____
_____
_____
_____
_____
_____
_____
_____
_____
_____
_____
_____
_____
_____
_____
_____
_____
_____
_____
_____
_____
_____
_____
_____

Today's Date: _____

What is your grief level from 0-10, with ten being the strongest? _____

What is your dominate feeling, emotion, or mood today?
_____

What are your thoughts today?

_____
_____
_____
_____
_____
_____
_____
_____
_____
_____
_____
_____
_____
_____
_____
_____
_____
_____
_____
_____
_____
_____
_____
_____
_____
_____
_____
_____
_____

Today's Date: _____

What is your grief level from 0-10, with ten being the strongest? _____

What is your dominate feeling, emotion, or mood today? _____

What are your thoughts today?

_____
_____
_____
_____
_____
_____
_____
_____
_____
_____
_____
_____
_____
_____
_____
_____
_____
_____
_____
_____
_____
_____
_____
_____
_____
_____
_____
_____
_____
_____
_____
_____

Today's Date: _____

What is your grief level from 0-10, with ten being the strongest? _____

What is your dominate feeling, emotion, or mood today?
_____

What are your thoughts today?

_____
_____
_____
_____
_____
_____
_____
_____
_____
_____
_____
_____
_____
_____
_____
_____
_____
_____
_____
_____
_____
_____
_____
_____
_____
_____
_____

Today's Date: _____

What is your grief level from 0-10, with ten being the strongest? _____

What is your dominate feeling, emotion, or mood today? _____

What are your thoughts today?

_____
_____
_____
_____
_____
_____
_____
_____
_____
_____
_____
_____
_____
_____
_____
_____
_____
_____
_____
_____
_____
_____
_____
_____
_____
_____
_____
_____
_____
_____

Words That Were Left Unspoken

Words That Were Left Unspoken

Special Notes and Remembrances

FROM THE AUTHOR

It has been a year and you have come a long way. Continue to pick yourself up and keep moving on your journey. As long as you are alive, the sun still rises for you and it also sets for you. You still have life in you and you must keep living it. May God's grace, peace, and strength carry you through.

~Lisa Mikell

Made in the USA
Middletown, DE
07 November 2019

78116371R00219